YOU CAN
BE
MORE
THAN
YOU ARE

T. Cecil Myers

YOU CAN
BE
MORE
THAN
YOU ARE

Word Books, Publisher
Waco, Texas

First Printing, June 1976
Second Printing, December 1976
First Paperback Printing, October 1978
Second Paperback Printing, July 1979

All Scripture quotations, unless otherwise noted, are from the
King James or Authorized Version of the Bible.

Quotations from the Revised Standard Version of the Bible (RSV)
are copyrighted 1946, 1952, © 1971, 1973 by the Division of
Christian Education of the National Council of the Churches
of Christ in the U.S.A., and are used by permission.

Grateful acknowledgment is made for the use of copyrighted
material from:

The Poetry of Robert Frost, "The Road Not Taken," edited by
Edward Connery Lathem. Copyright 1916, © 1969 by Holt,
Rinehart and Winston. Copyright 1944 by Robert Frost. Reprinted by permission of Holt, Rinehart and Winston, Publish-
ers, Jonathan Cape Ltd., and the Estate of Robert Frost.

Man of La Mancha, "The Impossible Dream (The Quest)"
by Joe Darion © MCMLXV Andrew Scott, Inc., Helena Music
Corp., and reprinted by permission of Sam Fox Publishing Company Inc.

Good Friday and Other Poems by John Masefield. Copyright 1915,
1916 by John Masefield, renewed 1943, 1944 by John Masefield
and reprinted by permission of Macmillan Publishing Co., Inc.
and The Society of Authors as the literary representative of the
Estate of John Masefield.

The Collected Poems of Laurence Housman, "A Prayer for the
Healing of the Wounds of Christ." Reprinted by permission of
the Executors of the Laurence Housman Estate and Jonathan
Cape Ltd.

ISBN #0-8499-2846-x
Library of Congress catalog card number: 76–2859
Printed in the United States of America

*This book is gratefully dedicated to
William Ragsdale Cannon
Resident Bishop of the Atlanta Area
of The United Methodist Church,
Scholar, Church Historian, Preacher
of the Gospel, Christian Gentleman,
and my friend and teacher*

Contents

Foreword

I have been the most fortunate of Methodist preachers. I have had six varied assignments during my ministry in the church. They have included being director of youth work for the annual conference, and pastor of five churches: a suburban church, an old downtown church, a medium-sized county seat church, and the largest United Methodist Church in the Southeast. For the past four years, I have served as senior minister of a 150-year-old church of 2300 members in a county seat—a college town of 60,000 people. Athens is a bustling city, made up of many kinds of people. It is a thrilling thing to serve as pastor in a city with the usual town-gown conflicts, the many social and educational opportunities, the black-white tensions, where football is absolutely king for eleven weeks each year, with 20,000 students, with hundreds of foreign students and their families giving an international flavor, with the usual struggles, political and otherwise, between old-timers and newcomers. What a great place and time to be alive! Athens is a city with a history, the only double-barreled cannon in the world, and the only tree on earth that owns itself!

Counseling has always been a vital part of my ministry. I have found time and desire to visit homes, hospitals, dormitories, sorority houses, fraternity houses, prisons, businesses, offices, and pizza parlors. I have prayed over hundreds of banquets, and made innumerable after-dinner speeches with indigestion. I count among my friends the very wealthy, the very poor, the educated and the ignorant, black and white,

American and foreigner, all kinds of people. I have never met a person I didn't like. Out of a varied, happy life has come the title of this little book: "You Can Be More Than You Are!" I believe that is true for every person. Perhaps the experiences that follow will convince someone of this truth.

There is more searching going on than I have ever known as evidenced by the identity crisis, the success syndrome, the constant mobility, the reality of a sudden death in a dormitory, an unexpected kindness, the necessity of finding a job, a nervous breakdown, a sometimes unconcerned church, questions of integrity and morality, choices in religion, new styles of living and dying. What a day to live. What a time to be more than you are.

The heart of the Christian faith is not a correct opinion about God, or a correct opinion about anything else for that matter. It is not the recitation of a creed on Sunday morning while half asleep, nor is it the proper answers to a set of questions by a preacher. *It is a personal relationship with a God who made himself known in Jesus, and whose spirit is still at work in the world saying "I am come that you might have life!"*

The Christian faith is practical, workable in the lives of all kinds of people. It is being willing to get hands dirty, feet muddy, to go out on dark nights and to far places to help. It works.

None of us lives up to capacity in any way. George Bernard Shaw once said, "Few people think more than two or three times a year. I have made an international reputation by thinking once or twice a week." Not only in thinking, but in every area of life we are content to operate far below capacity. We live in the cellars of the house of life when we might just as well live on at least the first floor, and maybe even the second. You can be more than you are. Five of the most hopeful words in the New Testament are "You are . . .

that you may . . ." (1 Pet. 2:9 rsv). You can be more than you are! I dare you to try it!

I am deeply grateful to Mrs. Harold Braswell, not only for preparing the manuscript but for all she does as secretary to make my work easier and more efficient.

T. Cecil Myers

You Can Be
More Than You Are

In preparation for this chapter read John 1:42.

Do you ever have the feeling that you are fully alive, thrillingly alive to the very fingertips? Or as Edward R. Murrow asked, "Are you living a life or an apology?" Albert Camus once said, "Man is the only creature who refuses to be what he is." I have come in this book to say that you can be more than you are. You can live with confidence!

One of the most thought-provoking scenes in the New Testament is in the first chapter of John. It is the story of Andrew, who heard Jesus himself, and began to follow him. Then he found his brother Simon. He said to him, "We have found the Messiah." And he brought him to Jesus. Jesus looked at Simon and said, " 'So you are Simon the son of John? You shall be called Cephas' (which means Peter)" (John 1:42 RSV). Here are five of the most hope-filled words in literature: "You are . . . you shall be." This whole chapter reveals the kind of people Jesus called to be his disciples.

13

They weren't different from us. We look back and attach
glory and strength to these early Christians. Believe me when
I say they were people just as we are people, with the same
longings, same desires, same sins, same failures, same weak-
nesses, same strengths. They were not a bigger breed; just
as ordinary as any of us. They were no better, no worse. Jesus
saw beneath the surface and saw possibilities. Wordsworth
put it:

> . . . saw into the depth of human souls,
> Souls that appeared to have no depth at all
> To careless eyes.
> —*Prelude, Book XIII*

Peter is a good example. He was intensely human. He was
a lovable character even in his blunders. His special mark
was his undependability. He was sudden and fickle and as
changing in mood as the sea from which he drew his living.
Jesus looked at him and said, "You are . . . you shall be."

Those who knew Peter must have doubted that he would
ever be a stone, as Jesus predicted. But one day they were at
Caesarea Philippi. Jesus asked them what people were saying
about him. They quoted what they had heard from folks.
Then Jesus said to them, "But who do you say that I am?"
Simon Peter replied, "You are the Christ, the Son of the
living God." And Jesus answered him, "Blessed are you,
Simon Bar-Jona! For flesh and blood has not revealed this
to you, but my Father who is in heaven. And I tell you, you
are Peter, and on this rock I will build my church, and the
powers of death shall not prevail against it" (Matt. 16:15-18
rsv). "Upon this rock." And it came out that way. At Pentecost Peter stood firm as a rock and preached a despised gospel
to a hateful crowd and three thousand of them were converted. He was crucified head downward, according to legend,

because he felt himself unworthy to be crucified as his Lord had been. "You are . . . you shall be."

We live in an extraordinary age! A man walked across the United States in seventeen minutes recently—*a hundred miles in the air!* Others have walked on the moon. Someone described a computer that will make 100,000 computations per minute. New planes are in the making that will fly twenty-one-hundred miles an hour with a payload of more than four hundred passengers. In medicine, in communications, in home building, in cooking, in just about every area of life there has been a revolution, making this the most extraordinary age man has ever known. A doctor told me recently that medical knowledge will be doubled in the next five years. I hope I live to the year 2000. It will be an amazing thing! We have watched miracles take place before our very eyes, things undreamed of even by a Jules Verne in the wildest science fiction books.

Great as these miracles are, there is yet a greater one—you can be more than you are. While we have done such marvelous things in science and manufacturing and the conquest of space, we have left the spirit of man the greatest undeveloped, unexplored area in all of life. The dark country of earth is the soul of man. How few people are really, thrillingly, tinglingly alive right down to their fingertips. Just as surely as we have made discoveries in science and all the other areas, so there are mighty discoveries waiting for us in the realm of the soul, the spirit of man. We pray a little prayer, "If I should die before I wake . . ." It ought to be, "If I should wake before I die . . ." Jonathan Swift used to say, "May you live all your life." Few of us ever do. We are made for greater things than we are getting. We can be more than we are. Here are three steps that will help us become more than we are.

First, get rid of your inner conflicts. Sir William Osler

once said, "At night, as I lay aside my clothes, I undress my soul too, and lay aside my sin. In the presence of God I lie down to rest and to waken a free man with a new life." We are learning the truth of the Bible verse, "The way of transgressors is hard" (Prov. 13:15). There is nothing that blights life as quickly or as completely as sin in our lives.

When I was a boy on the farm, I used to marvel at a little weed that grew profusely. It was a delicate, lacy plant that looked so beautiful in the early morning sun with dew on it. But it had a strange characteristic. If you touched it, it would close up. There is a little flower in Africa that is a thing of beauty. But if you touch it, it will wither immediately and drop from the plant. What a lesson for mankind. Personality was created in the image of God, looked upon and declared to be good. But one has only to let the awfulness of sin alienate him from God, and that beauty fades. Sometimes that personality dies before the master touch of recreative power can restore it. Nothing keeps us from confident living like sin in our lives.

Henry Ward Beecher used to tell of ships anchored in the bay, swinging in the tide as if they would follow the tide out to sea. But far beneath the surface they were anchored and could not move. So many souls sway heavenward, but cannot go because they are anchored to some secret sin.

There is no need for sin, any sin, to blight life. I stood beside a strange-looking little house in Galilee. A sign announced that this was the site of the home of Mary of Magdala. I wish we knew more about her. One day she was taken in the act of adultery. Her accusers dragged her to Jesus for his permission to stone her. He said that whoever of them was without sin might cast the first stone. He stooped and wrote in the sand. Her accusers disappeared, and when he looked up they were alone. He looked deep into her soul, perhaps the first time any man had ever looked at her with

love rather than lust. And when she said that no one remained to accuse her, Jesus said tenderly, "Neither do I
condemn you; go, and do not sin again" (John 8:11, RSV). And
she became a new person. She was a faithful disciple. She
was the first one to go to the tomb, for she had been forgiven
so much, and she had so much to be thankful for.

This same miracle of forgiveness can take place in you
right this minute. I like the song in Romans 7:24, 25 and
8:1. The words are autobiographical for me.

> O wretched man that I am!
> Who shall deliver me from the body of this death?
> I thank God through Jesus Christ. . . .
> There is therefore now no condemnation
>   to them which are in Christ Jesus.

Get rid of conflicts, the conflicts of sin, wrongdoing, hate,
lust, fear, wrong motives. Faith in our Lord removes these
sins and in their place gives a new life.

E. Stanley Jones tells of a fakir who came to an Indian
village declaring he could make gold. The villagers gathered
around him as he poured water in a tub and then, putting
some coloring matter into it, began to stir it with a stick
and to repeat mantrams. When their attention was diverted,
he let some gold nuggets slip down the stick. He poured off
the water, and there was the gold at the bottom. The villagers'
eyes bulged. The moneylender offered five hundred rupees
for the formula. The fakir explained minutely how to make
it and then added, "But you must not think of a red-faced
monkey as you stir or the gold won't come." The baniya
promised to remember what he was to forget. But try as hard
as he would the red-faced monkey was there before him,
spoiling everything. The gold would not come.

One does not gain the victorious life by fighting his indi-
vidual sins, nor by trying to forget them. It is a law of the

mind that whatever gets your attention gets you. If, therefore, your sins get your attention, then your sins will get you.
But when we yield our sins to Jesus, we are forgiven, given
a new heart, new attitudes, new purposes. You can be more
than you are.

Second, decide what you want out of life and go all out
for it. With inner conflicts removed, you are in position to
take a positive step in this direction. I have been making
speeches in high schools lately, and have asked the question,
"What do you want out of life?" It is amazing how many
young people, as well as adults, do not have an answer. Where
are you going? A survey showed that nine out of ten people
had no goals. Every person must have some definite goals in
life before he can accomplish anything. It isn't enough to
drift, to dream, to be apathetic.

I like Alvin Dark. He is a Christian and a member of the
Fellowship of Christian Athletes. In 1949 the Braves traded
him to the Giants. A cigarette company approached Dark and
a number of other players for a testimonial, offering them
$500 just for the use of their names. Dark refused, saying
that he didn't want to influence anyone to begin smoking or
drinking. He went on to say, "We are tempted to feel that
we are at the mercy of circumstances, but the fact is we are
the master of circumstances when we put our faith in Christ."
He knew what he wanted. He wanted to be a Christian and
he stuck to his goal. William Jennings Bryan said, "Destiny
is not a matter of chance. It is a matter of choice."

I like to go to Warm Springs, Georgia. I never tire of
thinking of the great man who once lived and died there.
When he was thirty-nine years old Franklin Delano Roosevelt
was stricken with polio and unbelievably crippled. Eleven
years later he was elected President of the United States.
When you walk around the Little White House you agree
with Thomas A. Edison that success is 2 percent inspiration

and 98 percent perspiration. What do you want out of life? Where are you going? Decide and then go for broke.

I remember talking with a man recently who has made a remarkable success in life. He said, "I never did have any kind of plan for my life. I just muddled along, hoping for the best. I was aimless. One day while reading my Bible I came across the story of the wise and foolish builders. That passage caused me to think seriously about my way of life. Out of my meditation came a plan, some goals, and a lot of determination." You can be more than you are if you have a plan and go for broke.

The third step is to use your faith. We misunderstand faith. The great trouble with our religion is that it has settled down, lost its zest, become a comfortable system of committees, denominations, and lightly accepted beliefs, in-herited traditions, political expediency. We put ourselves in black robes as preachers and lose touch with humanity. We call Christianity a system of doctrine, but it is more. We talk of social reform; it is more. We talk of a system of wor-ship and organizations, but it is even more. Jesus said, "I am come that they might have life, and that they might have it more abundantly" (John 10:10).

What is life? Vitality. Motion. Excitement. Enthusiasm. The Bible says, "In him was life." He said, "Because I live you shall live also." We have faith in the banker, the butcher, the candlestick maker. We trust all kinds of people we do not see. But we refuse to trust Jesus and follow him, when all the time this is the one faith that will make it possible for us to be alive. You have faith; I have faith. We just put it in the wrong things. Faith in Christ is the most transforming thing on earth. A businessman said to me recently, "There is no problem one cannot penetrate if he yields it to the illumination of God."

A preacher went to visit a Naval Air Station. The officer in charge told him: "A most important lesson we have to teach our pilots is how to live with relaxed power. In this business of combat flying a pilot can never know when he may have to meet a crisis, and he must be ready and relaxed at all times." Flying and living aren't any different. Francis Tarkenton of the Minnesota Vikings said, "I believe he enables those who trust him to do their best." And so he does. The early disciples excite me. They had no organization, no prestige, no money. But they told people how to live. And they did it in simple language: "Believe in the Lord Jesus, and you will be saved" (Acts 16:31 RSV). That was their message, and you can't improve on it. Put your trust in Jesus, follow his way, put into practice what he said and taught by example, and you'll find yourself more fully alive than you ever dreamed.

Get rid of conflicts. Decide what you want out of life. Use your faith. What a simple formula to help us become more than we are. "You are . . . you shall be!"

2

Who Will Answer?

In preparation for this chapter read Matthew 6:5-13.

Some time ago there was a popular song entitled, "Who Will Answer?" It had a lot of questions about life, death, war, romance, family, and ended each of them with the plaintive question, "Who will answer?" And that raises a very interesting question: will anybody answer? Is there really any use in asking? One of the questions I am asked most frequently by young and old, in church and out, is about prayer. Is there anything to it? How does it work? I believe we can be more than we are, through prayer.

We moderns are giants in terms of physical power. How puny we are in other ways. We are precocious technologically but we are adolescent spiritually. We have learned to fly the air like birds, to swim the sea like fish, and to burrow the ground like moles. But we have not yet learned to walk the earth like men. Our spiritual powers are not great enough to control our physical discoveries. We are like pygmies paddling in mud puddles, while God's great ocean of power is all before us. We have learned to make labor-saving devices, but we have not yet learned how to lay hold on the kind of power that will enable us to use these devices in the right way. It is a dangerous thing to have power, but not the character to use it rightly. We are exhausted, fretful, angular. We are in difficulty in every area of our living: family, politics, education, economics. Youth have problems. We cry out of the deep distresses of our inner being for help. Who will answer?

There is no power like prayer. Dr. Alexis Carrel once said, "The most powerful form of energy one can generate is prayer. Prayer is a force as real as terrestrial gravity. Prayer like radium is a luminous and self-generating form of energy." There is a power greater than the atom locked up in the human heart. That power can control the atom. It is spiritual power and is released through prayer. We work, we think, we push, we shove. These are the commonly accepted ways of getting ahead. Prayer is thought of as something special, to be used at funerals, weddings, and baptisms, and made by the pastor in the pulpit. It is something special for special days, Sunday-go-to-meeting stuff apart from our daily lives. It is saved for the sanctuary. The elimination of prayer from man's common daily experience is tragic. It compels us to bear the burdens of life alone. No wonder we turn to pills and alcohol, and have nervous breakdowns, and commit suicide.

A lot of us continue the form of prayer, but millions do not expect anything to happen when they pray. They could stop doing what they call praying without any noticeable effect on their lives. Their so-called prayers do not affect their lives, nor do they expect them to do so. Prayer for so many of us, preacher and layman alike, is unreal, or at least not real power. It is a meaningless motion through which we go until we get utterly weary of the whole thing and give it up as bad business.

It is still childish for many of us. I suppose it is all right to teach children to pray, "Now I lay me down to sleep. I pray thee, Lord, my soul to keep. If I should die before I wake, I pray thee, Lord, my soul to take. Amen." But even if it is all right to teach that to children, it is not all right for thirty- or fifty- or seventy-year-old people to keep on praying it. Many of us have not yet progressed out of the very first, elemental stages of prayer. So it has little meaning for us.

Or some of us really doubt the value of prayer. We look on it as autosuggestion, or a psychological gimmick, or a tool of the preacher. Mark Twain's Huck Finn sums it up pretty well for us:

> Miss Watson, she took me in the closet and prayed, but nothing come of it. She told me to pray every day, and whatever I asked for I would get it. But it warn't so. I tried it. Once I got a fish line, but no hooks. It warn't any good to me without hooks. I tried for the hooks three or four times, but somehow I couldn't make it work. By and by, one day, I asked Miss Watson to try for me, but she said I was a fool. She never told me why, and I couldn't make it out no way.
>
> I set down one time back in the woods, and had a long think about it. I says to myself, if a body can get anything they pray for why don't deacon Winn get back the money he lost on pork? Why can't the widow get back her silver snuff box that was stole? Why can't Miss Watson fat up? No, I say to myself, there ain't nothing in it.

And a lot of us feel that way, even some of us who have never quite given up the forms of prayer.

Some of us use prayer only when we are in trouble. A little boy climbed up on a high, sharp roof. He lost his footing and began to slide toward the edge. He began to pray, "O Lord, save me! O Lord, save me! O Lord . . . never mind, I caught my britches on a nail." Prayer becomes a useful tool in every time of trouble.

Or some of us turn to prayer only when we want something, and our own ingenuity fails us. A preacher out visiting asked a six-year-old boy if he prayed every night. "No sir," replied the little fellow. "Some nights I don't want nothing." And we occasionally find ourselves in the spot of not wanting anything.

Prayer has not become for us what James Montgomery had in mind when he wrote:

> Prayer is the soul's sincere desire,
> Unuttered or expressed,
> The motion of a hidden fire
> That trembles in the breast.

I am interested in going beyond where we are now in prayer. I believe we can be more than we are.

One night, Marie and Pierre Curie were lying in bed talking. They were discussing the fact that everything in the universe was made up of some combination of the eighty-six elements which science had discovered at that time. Everything animate and inanimate was in some way composed of these elements. Suddenly, Marie said, "Pierre, just suppose out there beyond what we now know there should be another element, something science had not dreamed of." Pierre, according to the story, jumped out of bed, danced around the room saying over and over, "Just suppose out there beyond . . ." Later Pierre was killed in an accident, but Marie went on with her research, and discovered that there was something out there beyond. She discovered radium which has become such a blessing to the human race. There's always more out there beyond the mind's horizon and the heart's horizon. So let's go beyond where we are now in prayer!

What is prayer? Let me tell you first what it is not. It is not begging; it is not the refuge of the weak and sissy; it is not bending God's will to my way and will; it is not occasional exercise to which to resort when all else has failed; it is not magic to take the place of work; it is not an optional subject in the curriculum of life. It is not getting God to do for us what we ought to be doing for ourselves.

One day a girl who was very much overweight came to see me. She wanted a husband. She said for a long while she had prayed twice every day for a husband. I told her that God couldn't answer a prayer like that by himself. She ought to get busy and lose thirty pounds, stop chewing gum like a cud-chewing cow in public, get something done about that stringy hair, read some books and try to learn the art of interesting conversation, learn some of the social graces of life. Then having done all she could, submit it all to God. She stomped out mad as a wet hen. I never could understand what made her so mad. But a year or so went by, and once when I was making a speech somewhere, this very attractive woman came up and just stood in front of me and said nothing. It slowly dawned on me that this was the woman I had insulted. But it had worked. People pray to God that they won't have cancer, and go right on smoking the cancer stick! If prayer is anything it is reasonable, sensible.

Well then, what is prayer? I can sum it up in one short story. When I was about fourteen I had a Sunday school teacher who was a big man in every way. He taught me to swim. No, what really happened was, he picked me up by the seat of the pants and the nape of the neck and threw me into muddy Chickamauga Creek. He simply said, "Now swim!" After watching the blue sky turn muddy red twice, I began to kick and paddle and that was how I learned to swim.

Bob heard that Kagawa was to be in Chattanooga and he thought his Sunday school boys ought to hear this Japanese Christian. So on a Sunday afternoon we went to hear the man, hoping that afterwards there'd be a trip to the Krystal hamburger place. I shall never forget how Kagawa looked. He was very short of stature, wore very thick glasses, but he spoke in a positive way. When he had finished Bob thought we ought to meet him, so he took us backstage and we all shook hands. Several people were asking him questions, and one was simply, "What is prayer?" This great man, honored by his own nation, revered by Christians everywhere said simply, "Prayer is surrender." I'll never forget that simple, short definition of prayer. When we think of surrender we think of a yellow streak right up the back, or cowardice. But in this case, surrender means the yielding of one's spirit to the spirit of God to cooperate with him in accomplishing his will for our lives. It is like the yielding of the flower to sun, rain, soil for growth and beauty, the yielding of the mind of the student to the process of education for learning, the yielding of the light bulb to the dynamo for brilliance. It is the yielding up of my spirit to the love and power of God for the strength I need for living every day.

Anne Morrow Lindbergh put it beautifully in her book, *Gift from the Sea* (Random House): "One should lie empty, open, choiceless as a beach waiting for a gift from the sea." And that is what prayer really is!

How do you come by a vital prayer life? Some assume that to make commitment of life to Christ ushers in a vital prayer life. Not so. Commitment is the beginning. A vital life of prayer is the result of commitment plus some other things.

It is not had for nothing. I was walking across the air terminal in Atlanta recently and was fascinated by a little boy who was going from one telephone to another pulling down the coin return lever to see if anyone had forgotten a dime. He was trying to get something for nothing. To "receive . . . a Presence, a presence as power" as Martin Buber says, "is no small thing and is not had for nothing." How is prayer-power achieved?

(1.) There must be discipline of time, place, and diligence. Paul said, "Pray without ceasing" (1 Thess. 5:17) and "Be instant in season, out of season" (2 Tim. 4:2). But there must be something more specific. There is but one way to mastery in anything: discipline. Ben Hogan was playing in a golf tournament years ago. He was on the last hole. He sliced off to the right, two hundreds yards from the pin. The way to the green lay through a narrow passage in the trees. He took his 2-iron and drove the ball within ten feet of the pin, and won the tournament. When someone congratulated him, he said, "I didn't make that shot just now. I have been practicing it since I was twelve." Jesus said, "Because strait is the gate, and narrow is the way, which leadeth unto life, and few there be that find it" (Matt. 7:14).

Carl Michaelson once said, "You never know about prayer until you pray." The only way to pray is to pray whether you feel like it or don't. Nobody has more of a struggle with this than I. I can remember the alarm going off in years gone by, groping around in the dark for my clothes, and struggling into the study muttering, "Lord, this isn't fair to my family for me to be up disturbing their sleep just so I can have prayer." So back to bed I would go. I have awakened on cold mornings and snuggled down into the blankets assuring myself that God could hear prayers originating from anywhere. This may be praying, but it produces no power. Since I began a regular time and place for prayer, things have been different. We achieve perfection by the discipline of practice. A singer sings by practice. An artist becomes perfect by practice. Thomas Edison did his experiments, some thousands of times, before he achieved the answer he sought. So have a time, a place, a method, and stay with it day after day, whether you feel like it or not.

Do you know how a man becomes a public speaker? Here is one way. Fill your mouth with marbles, then begin to speak. The first day, you take out one marble. You go on talking. The second day you take out another marble, then on the third day another, and when you have lost all your marbles you become a public speaker. You become a public speaker by practice—long, hard, tedious practice. Likewise, there is no other way to perfection in prayer.

(2.) Our prayers ought to be simple and natural. Rufus Jones describes God as one "whose being opens into ours, and ours into his, who is the very life of our lives, the matrix of our personality; and there can be no separation between us unless we make it ourselves." If this is the kind of friendship we can know with God our prayers can be simple and natural.

Daddy Butters was a teacher in one of our theological schools up East. When he prayed in chapel, his face would light up as if he were talking with a friend. The students called him "Daddy" Butters. He didn't mind. He told his class of the troubles he and his wife had about prayer. She was a stern, rigid sort of Christian who thought that the only way to pray was on one's knees by the bed. It gets very cold in New England, and she was a fresh-air fiend. At bedtime, she would open the windows, and with the north wind whistling through the room, would kneel and pray. Often she would discover when she opened her eyes that Daddy Butters had slipped into bed. She'd always say, "George, have you said your prayers?" He'd reply, "I'm saying them now." "George," she'd insist, "you get out of bed and say your prayers in proper manner." Painfully, he'd obey. But he said, "My prayers were then short and to the point." To this man, God was a friend, one who could be approached at any time, anywhere. He lived his life with God, and his prayers were simple and natural. You don't have to pose before God. Just say what you feel and say it like you were talking with somebody.

(3.) Be honest with God. God already knows us, our inner life. Prayer leaves us naked before him. Be perfectly honest. Keith Miller says in *The Taste of New Wine* (Word Books) that once his prayers had been filled with dishonest words. Let me quote him: "I had always started out by saying, 'God, I adore you,' whether I really did or not that morning. Now I could say, when it was true, 'Lord, I am sorry but I am tired of you today. I am tired of trying to do your will all the time, and I'd like to run away and raise hell!' But I could also continue, 'But Lord, forgive me for this willfulness; and even though I don't feel like it, I ask you to lead me today to be your person and to do your will!' " This is honesty!

A man walked into my office some time ago and threw a quarter on my desk and said it was the price of his soul. I was startled and asked what he meant. "Exactly what I say. I stole it out of the cash register at the store, and I've been doing it for ten years. I tried to persuade myself at first that I wasn't paid enough and that I had it coming to me. I excused myself that it was just for carfare. But today I saw myself for what I am, a sneaking thief, and I want to be rid of this guilt." We knelt, and he prayed, not "O Lord, forgive me for being a sinner" but he cried out, "O Lord, forgive me for being a sneaking thief." He got his forgiveness, and we went together to his employer and told the story. He made restitution as best he could, and today is a happy employee of that same store. Be honest in prayer.

(4.) Be specific in your praying. I hear people say, "O Lord, forgive us all our sins." You can hide a lot of sins under that and they won't ever see the light of day, or forgiveness either. What sins? If you are a thief, say so. If you have committed adultery, say so. If you have refused help when somebody needed you, say so. "O Lord, bless our missionaries." What are their names? "O Lord, bless our preacher." What is his problem? I like to pray for people and situations by name, and I think it produces some power to do it that way.

(5.) Pray with faith. What do you expect to happen when you pray? Do you remember the story in Matthew 17? A man brought his boy to the nine disciples, who waited at the foot of the mountain while Jesus was up there with Peter, James, John. He wanted the boy healed. The disciples tried all they knew to work the miracle. It wouldn't come out right. Later, after Jesus had healed the boy, the disciples asked, "How come? Why couldn't we do that?" And Jesus replied simply, "Because of your unbelief. . . ."

I was at a conference once where the preachers were making oral reports on their work. One young man reported that there had been no additions to his church either by profession of faith or by transfer that year. The presiding officer, an older man, stopped him and said, "Son, at the beginning of the year, did you expect that there would be any additions to your church this year?" What do you really expect to happen when you pray, or are you just mumbling words to carry on a tradition. Believe that something will happen and, brothers and sisters, something will happen.

Prayer drives us beyond ourselves. Somehow, we find that we are persons with powers we never dreamed possible. We not only are enabled to work through our own problems and make a creative contribution to the life we now live, but we move over into the circle of family and friends, then out across barriers to involvement in the lives of all kinds of people. Prayer is the most wonderful relationship on earth. It gets us outside ourselves, and gives life the enlargement, the horizon, the power that God wants for us all.

I have learned that prayer is not a way to get God to do things for me. It is a direction of life, a presence, and a power. It is focusing one's deepest and most personal attention on God. When we do that increasingly, our wills and actions will be more and more aligned with his until finally all our lives are lived with the mark of his love and compassion. Then things get done.

Uncle Charlie Teasley, who lived in Philadelphia until his death in 1954, told me a story of a black preacher. He had members living all over the city, and one of them made his living with a team of mules, plowing, hauling, and doing odd jobs. He lived on the edge of the city, and his house fronted on a divided boulevard, with flowers, shrubs, trees, in the center of the street. One day the preacher went to visit this member. He walked up on the front porch, knocked at the door, and found no answer. The door was closed and locked. He went around back, and his eyes were met by trash, debris, junk, accumulated over the years. The backyard was a mess. He looked and the back door was wide open. He shouted as he mounted the steps, "No, no! You can't keep the back door of your house open on all the trash and refuse in the backyard, and the front door closed on the beauty of the boulevard!" Friend, you and I can't keep the back door of our lives open on all the trash, the happenings of the day, the problems, and troubles of life, and the front door closed on the power of heaven. It just won't work. Who will answer? God will!

3

"My God! I Don't Know How to Die!"

In preparation for this chapter read Philippians 1.

I am going to die. So are you. As soon as a man is born he is old enough to die. We think death comes to the old, or at least to someone else. It comes to every man. Recently, I have performed several funerals. One was a three-year-old; the other an eighty-year-old. Not long ago a young woman was in an automobile accident. She was hurt, but not badly. When she got better, she came to see me. Her opening statement was "My God! I don't know how to die!" Webb Garrison, in his book *Creative Imagination in Preaching* (Abingdon) tells of one of the cultural institutions in the Midwest—the country auction. When a householder dies, his heirs bring together his household goods, and they invite the public to come look and buy. At such an auction, one might see four horses, twelve cows, thirty sheep. There would be scrap metals, some wire, maybe a thirty-gallon copper kettle in which apple butter was made. There might be a brass bed, tables piled high with glassware and bric-a-brac, an old tintype of Grandma. Then he writes: ". . . the country auction points to a basic truth: one day soon, very soon, as the cosmic clock ticks, all will be called to appear before the Father. Relatives will hire an auctioneer and set up a hotdog stand in the tool shed, with root beer and coffee for the nice people who will buy the apple-butter kettle for $14.75, and Grandma's tintype for a dime."

I can hear you saying, "Don't be so morbid." I'm not morbid. I'm going to die. So are you. And we'd better face up to it. We can be more than we are if we face up to death realistically, and see it, not as an enemy, but as a potential friend. No person knows how to live until he begins to know how to die. Now I'll admit I have trouble feeling what Paul was feeling when he said, "For me to live is Christ, and to die is gain. If it is to be life in the flesh, that means fruitful labor for me. Yet which I shall choose I cannot tell" (Phil. 1:21-22 RSV). He was having a hard time making up his mind whether it was better to live or die. I want to live! I'm in no hurry to die.

There's an old bewhiskered story that illustrates my feelings on the matter. A preacher met two little boys. He spoke to them, then said, "Boys, would you like to go to heaven?" "Yes, sir!" one responded brightly. "No, sir," said the other honestly. Surprised, the preacher asked, "Son, do you mean that eventually you don't want to go to heaven?" "Eventually," replied the boy, "but I thought you were getting up a load to go today." I'm with him.

I love life. I'd like to live until the year 2000 just to see what will be new, and hopefully to see the end of war, and racial tension, and hunger. I am anxiously awaiting the next moon shot. I love life, and beauty, and friends, and all that is going on in these challenging times. But I am going to die, and I'd better face up to that simple fact. I'll be a better person when I do.

We push death down. In fact, death is not discussed in any rational way in polite company. We make jokes about it, but it is too shocking for polite company. We never tell our children about it. Paul uses more common sense than we do. He talks about death as we would a flight from Atlanta to San Francisco. This is a death-denying age. Man is the only creature that knows he is going to die, and he tries to forget it. This is why he is so poorly equipped to face it. We see the rejection of the fact of death in countless ways. We emphasize youth to avoid the fact of aging. Nothing is more pathetic to me than a seventy-year-old woman with a mini-skirt, knobby knees and a shape like a sack of potatoes trying to convince the world that she is still young. Men join clubs to indulge in teen-age horseplay that would make such teen-age activity look like the antics of a three-year-old. Advertisers play on this idea too: by picturing young people in advertisements of drinks, foods, cars, etc., they seem to say "you buy these things and you'll stay young."

I like the story of the middle-aged man who sets out to play tennis. He gets all set. His spirit says to him, "Now hit the ball like a bullet, then rush up to the net for a return, get all set to slam it down his throat, stand on tiptoe, blazing eyes, breathing heavy. . . ." And his body says, "Who, me?"

We try to hide death by not going to funerals very often. Most funerals are so anonymous that you can't tell who is being buried. I have a preacher friend who tells of a funeral he had. He was late getting there, and didn't know the person whose funeral he was to have. He didn't even know whether it was a man or a woman. The people were already in the church when he got there. He walked breathlessly down the aisle, and in a vain attempt to find out if it was a male or female, he leaned over to a relative and said, "Brother or sister?" The relative whispered back, "Neither. Cousin!"

We once felt that to have a general sort of funeral would make things easier for the family. To be sure we ought to revolt against some of the crudities of the Victorian funeral. We ought to leave off unsuitable music, long wordy sermons, and we ought to leave the casket closed. But the funeral service ought to be more: it ought to be a service of worship to Almighty God, a service of celebration, and it ought to have some content to it. A long sermon is out of place, but certainly a Christian meditation for the benefit of the family and friends ought to be included to help lead men toward God as Father of all.

We treat grief as if it were an immoral thing. "I must be brave and not cry," a woman said to me recently. I asked "Why?" Grief of the right sort is healthy, even noble. It is not a sign of weakness. It ought not to be uncontrollable, and will not be if we are Christian. But to shed tears is not just human, it is divine. Jesus stood before the grave of his closest friend, with others of his closest friends and the Bible says, "Jesus wept." We try to obscure death by making grief seem wrong.

I like what Herman Feifel, the psychologist, said in his book *The Meaning of Death* (McGraw-Hill): "Our ways of living and dying make it quite possible to deny that death exists—until it proves its existence near at hand." Death is so deeply disturbing because we deny it or try to hide it. When it comes to us, or to a loved one, it comes as a shock for which we have made no preparation.

We need death to give meaning to life. It is hard enough to fill a limited number of days with significance, let alone be faced with an infinite number of days. Life would become intolerable without death. You don't really know how to live until you learn how to die. Without the blessing of death all urgency would go out of human choices and life would become a perpetual bore. The value of prolonging life is questionable unless we discover ways to give life meaning and purpose. A student once remarked: "I have no reason for living. Many seem to do well without one, earning money to have a good time, but a man needs a reason, and I haven't one." Paul said, "For to me to live is Christ, and to die is gain" (Phil. 1:21). He meant that with Christ in the heart, life made sense and death made no difference. Through our senses we may gain everything we need for living except one: a reason. It is pitiful to go through the motions of living but never live. Somehow, the knowledge that we are going to die, that our days are not without limit, makes our search for meaning more diligent.

There is another way in which death gives meaning to life. Death provides an escape from intolerable conditions. It is the way God has provided for us to leave these old shells we call body when we are through with them. Death comes as a friend when one has been sick for months, and strength is depleted and the body is wasted away. "Precious in the sight of the Lord is the death of his saints," said the Psalmist (116:15).

John Quincy Adams met a friend on the street one day. The friend said, "How do you do, Mr. Adams?" Elderly Mr. Adams replied, "John Quincy Adams is very well, thank you, but the house in which he is living is falling to pieces. Times and seasons have nearly destroyed it. I think John Quincy Adams will soon have to move out. But he himself is very well, sir." So God has planned wisely. The fact of death gives meaning to life. A wise man said, "So teach us to number our days that we may apply our hearts unto wisdom." He meant that we are to realize the shortness of this life, the certainty of death, and so make our days here precious.

The great fear of death lies in the unknown. Dr. Gardner

Murphy of the Menninger Foundation calls fear of death "the fear of the unknown." What we don't know about is frightening. I remember when I was a boy we lived about a mile from town. Sometimes in late afternoon mother would send me to the store. Often it would be dark when I returned. When I left the lighted streets of the village, everything took on new meaning. Every stump became a spook, every tree hid an evil spirit, a demon lurked in every fence corner, and every strange sound sent chills up my spine. The next day, in daylight, there was no fear, for the stumps and trees and fence corners and sounds showed up for what they really were. Or, if my dad happened to be with me at night, the stumps weren't a problem.

Nothing is more unknown than what lies beyond death. There is no way to make it known. Anyone who purports to know what lies beyond death is a fraud, a charlatan. We make guesses, but it is futile to describe literally heavenly bliss, or the punishments of hell. Harps, wings, golden streets, brimstone, everlasting fire mean little to us. We don't understand the Book of Revelation because we are literal-minded; we think like engineers instead of like mystics or poets. We can't describe the furniture of heaven, or the desolation of hell.

There is one thing that is better than descriptions, and that is trust. The unknown does not need to be known to lose its terrors. Many things are unknown to a child, for example: his first day at school, his first airplane ride, his first visit to the department store. These things don't terrify him because he has learned to trust his parents. He counts on the faithfulness of those he knows and so feels safe.

Take an operation, for example. We do not have to be terrified of the first operation. We can trust the doctor and feel safe. I heard of a man who had his first operation. When he regained consciousness, all the shades were drawn and the room was dark. The doctor came in, and the man asked him why the shades were drawn. The doctor replied, "There's a big fire raging right up the street, and I didn't want you to wake up and think the operation had been a failure."

We trust, and feel safe. Trust was Paul's secret. He did not speak of life after death as if he could name the streets of heaven. The one thing that mattered to him was that whether he was in life or death, he was with Christ. This companionship could not be destroyed. He would not be left alone no matter what came or went—that was all he needed to know. The fear of the unknown was removed for him because he trusted.

How do you get ready to die? It is a common error to think that eternal life begins when one dies. Eternal life is not out yonder somewhere. Eternal life is fellowship with God. It begins now. Every person must live in two worlds. Eternal life, the heavenly life, begins when one commits his life to Jesus Christ. That life is never interrupted thereafter. Death can't interrupt it. Death then becomes simply the way ordained by God for our passage from one stage of life to another. We do not stop loving, or growing just because we die. Why do many people come close to death and panic? Because they haven't prepared. I listened to an old salt talk about his experiences in World War I. One was especially interesting. They were in mid ocean. An enemy sub was sighted. He said it was almost amusing, had it not been so pathetic, to see men reaching for their New Testaments, trying to find something to hold on to and to help. When the danger passed, they put away their New Testaments until another emergency. No wonder we are afraid to die.

Jesus demonstrated the way to die. On the cross, he said to his Father, "Father, into thy hands I commend my spirit" (Luke 23:46). What an example of trust. What a way to die. Then he said to his disciples: "Let not your heart be troubled:

ye believe in God, believe also in me" (John 14:1). Our best approach to death is a commitment of life to Jesus, so that life for us becomes a growing, maturing fellowship with him.

Dr. John D. Verdery in his book *It's Better to Believe* (M. Evans) says that death is one of the human experiences which is handled better by someone who believes than by someone who does not. Hugh Walpole in his novel *The Inquisitor* has the bishop talking about death as it comes to him: "I see God's beauty burning through the veil of outward things—the past, the present—we are all in God's hands—God who knows nothing of time and who holds us in his arms, knowing that our sorrow is only the prelude to a deeper knowledge of his love. This knowledge prepares us to die."

There is a fascinating story in Dr. Halford Luccock's stimulating book *Communicating the Gospel* (Harper Brothers). A chaplain has officiated at a mass burial for eleven men who had been killed in one company. The day was dark and dreary, the skies dripped moisture. The chaplain finished the words, and their friends just stood in the drenching rain, somehow unable to move away or shake off the feeling of desperation. Then it happened: a little redheaded fellow, the company cook, began to sing: "There's a land that is fairer than day, and by faith we can see it afar; and the Father waits over the way, to . . ." How do you prepare to die? You begin now to live.

What is heaven like? Who knows. The idea of heaven as an endless church service has long since lost its appeal. The hymn that says heaven is a place where "congregations ne'er break up and sabbaths have no end" is no longer sung. We can barely make it for an hour on Sunday mornings, and most of us just can't take another hour on Sunday nights. You should hear the complaints if I go five minutes beyond twelve o'clock on Sunday mornings. That means the Methodists lose the foot race with the Baptists and Presbyterians for Morrison's Cafeteria. Some people never hear the benediction. For their information, that is the little prayer at the very, very end of the service. Heaven is not some kind of monastery, or a retirement home. No, whatever else it is, I think it will be a state of continued and continual growth.

There is no more beautiful passage in the Bible than John 14. One translation makes part of it read, "In my Father's house are many mansions . . ." (v. 2). I'm really not interested in mansions, what with the price of heat, lights, and upkeep. Another translates it, "In my Father's house are many stations . . ." That implies growth, progress, opportunity for adventure, abundant living. What encouragement for those who never quite arrived in this life, who died before they could paint the picture, or build the house, or write the poem. We don't know what heaven is like, but Paul settled the issue for me when he wrote, "O death, where is thy sting? O grave, where is thy victory?" (1 Cor. 15:55). There is no fear of death now, only hope for life beyond for those who themselves have experienced the resurrection. No wonder Dietrich Bonhoeffer could say as he approached death, "This is the end, but for me it is the beginning of life" (*Life Together,* Harper Brothers). The next day he was hanged at Flossenburg.

Last year my wife, Elizabeth, and I were in the northeastern part of Virginia browsing in a little county courthouse. I came across an old copy of *Barker's Almanac.* Years ago it was issued by the manufacturer of medicines for cattle and horses. In it was a great big puzzle for the children to work on. It showed a little boy standing beside a giant tree deep in the forest. In the background was a house. Beneath the picture were the instructions: "This little boy is lost. His father is looking for him. Puzzle: find the lad's father." It was quite a puzzle. No matter which way I turned it, there was no sign of the father. I worked with it for quite a while. Then laid it aside and went on looking for some other papers. Then I came back and just glanced at the picture, and there plain as the nose on my face was the outline of the father. Now I could see nothing else. The irregular sky-line formed his head and shoulders. The branches of trees made his body, and the tree trunks were his legs. He was so immense that he was all out of proportion to the size of the boy or the house. He was the whole picture itself. I missed him, because I was not looking for so great a person.

In thinking about death, we look behind every tree and shrub for some sign of God's presence. "He must be here somewhere," we console ourselves. And he is here, not some-where, but everywhere. He is the picture. We do not see him because he is all out of proportion to the little being for whom we have been searching to put in our little house, which our little minds have conceived to be his home. God is; he is all in all. Death is the experience by which we enter more com-pletely into the life of God. Why be afraid? When you know God, you know how to die. That knowledge makes us more than we are!

4

Tips for Tycoons: Slow Down, Man!

In preparation for this chapter read Isaiah 26:3; 40:28-31.

Tomorrow, I have at least one hundred things to do. You thought preachers work only one day each week. There is Sunday's sermon to work on, the tape for the telephone ministry to change, a staff meeting to attend, correspondence to answer, the publicity to prepare for the newspapers, some work to do on the new book, and a book to read in preparation for the reading club. There are the visitors from today's service and some inactive members to contact. There is some gardening to do at home, and the lawn needs attention. There is work to do on speeches for some forthcoming engagements. Some time must be set aside for the family. There seem to be more than one hundred things to do. How do I get them done?

I understand people who say the pressures of life are too much, and who feel they are cracking under the strain of today, and are fearful of tomorrow. However, there is a good kind of tension. A watch is of no value without a mainspring.

The mainspring is of no value without tension. Life would be flat and tasteless if we didn't have that something in us to make us want to get up and accomplish. The pressures around us need not be bad if we learn how to handle them without fretting. Every person can be more than he is by using life's strains and pressures in the right way.

Dr. Hans Selye of Montreal points out that chronic emotional stress brings on all kinds of illnesses and disabilities. All sickness has a common factor, whether it is an ordinary cold, heart disorder, arthritis, cancer, or just that "sick feeling." He thinks illness is caused by chemical imbalance in the body, and that is caused by constant stress and strain. Chemical balance is controlled by three very small glands, weighing less than an ounce: the two adrenals, and the pituitary. The hormones secreted by these glands have great influence on body balance. If we rush around, live constantly under pressure, are nervous and anxious, these little fellows work valiantly to keep balance, but often they can't keep pace. So the result is high blood pressure, hypertension, a heart disorder, the common cold, or something else. Continued stress breaks the machinery down. Though the apparent cause of illness is infection, actually it is a breakdown in the hormonal-adaptation machinery brought on by the strains and stresses of daily living. Doctors can do much at the physical level with tranquilizers, but nothing permanent can be done without getting at the root cause. We can do a lot with germ-caused diseases. We still know very little about the stress-caused diseases.

The prevailing American malady is hypertension, anxiety, nervousness. Too many people are dying too young. The worst enemies of American men and women of responsibility are heart disorders, nervous diseases, emotional breakdowns; and these are not germ caused, but stress caused.

A drug salesman told me recently that Americans consume nineteen million sleeping pills every night, and that annually we use eleven million pounds of aspirin. We average fifty aspirin each year per person, and one brand is just as good as another. Our patron saint is Saint Vitus. A woman said to her doctor, "Doctor, help me, I'm all run down." He replied calmly, "You aren't all run down, you are all wound up." No wonder the twentieth century has been dubbed "the Aspirin Age," "the Age of Anxiety," "the Sleeping Pill Century."

At one point or another all of us get caught up in the stresses of living and need help. Here are some major causes of stress.

There's too much going on. A Frenchman came to the United States years ago. He commented that Americans are crazy. They have invented a chair they call a "rocking chair" in which they can move while sitting down. Someone has said there are three great killers: the clock, the calendar, and the telephone.

When James Garfield was president of Hiram College in Ohio, he received a letter from a father asking if the course of study couldn't be shortened from four years. President Garfield replied that it could. "But it all depends on what you want to make of your son. When God wants to make an oak tree, he takes hundreds of years. But it only takes two months to make a squash."

I watch students at the University of Georgia go to school around the year, take as many hours as the law allows, work day and night to get through, and wind up with a nervous breakdown. We think we are living when we fill every day and night of our calendar with engagements and activities. Our calendars may be full and our lives totally empty.

A man from Texas walked up to the ticket counter at the

airport one day and said, "Give me a ticket!" "Where to?" asked the salesperson. "Anywhere," bellowed the pompous Texan, "I've got business all over." One requirement for membership in the Coronary Club is never say no to any request—always say yes!

We live too fast. Just look at our verbs: they are all action, fast action. We leap out of bed; we gulp our coffee; we bolt our food; we dash to town; we hurry into the office; we rush out for lunch; we wade through appointments; we whiz home; we drop dead. We live with such impatience. At one time if you wanted to go somewhere, you'd catch a stagecoach. If you missed one, there'd probably be another along in three weeks. But I saw a man get mad the other day just because he missed a section of a revolving door. The shortest period of time known to man is that space between the time the traffic light turns green and the fool behind you honks his horn.

Rome is a town in northwest Georgia. There is a time change at the Georgia-Alabama line, and a few miles over in Alabama is the town of Center. One day a man came to the Greyhound bus station in Rome and asked if there was a bus to Center, Alabama. The ticket agent told him there was a bus that left at six o'clock. "What time does it get to Center?" asked the man. "It get's there at six o'clock. Can I sell you a ticket?" The man thought about it for a long time, then said thoughtfully, "No, but you can let me stand here and watch that bus take off." One of the requirements for membership in the Coronary Club is to do everything as fast as possible.

Another cause of stress is worry. We need to distinguish between normal precautions and fretful worry. Certainly we ought to be afraid of fire, railroad crossings, poison. We ought to make preparation for living today and tomorrow. But there is a difference between fretful worry and intelligent concern. Jesus told his disciples not to be anxious. Nowhere did he tell them not to make careful preparation for living. We fret and fume our lives away. Somewhere I saw a worry survey:

40% of the things we worry about never happen
30% are in the past and can't be helped
12% concern the affairs of others that aren't our business
10% are about sickness, either real or supposed
 8% are worth worrying about

I visited a man in the hospital recently. He is a chronic worrier. Someone in his room commented, "If he doesn't have anything to worry about, that worries him." One fellow commented, "I have so many worries that if anything new came along it would be two weeks before I could get to it."

Work rarely kills. In fact, all things being equal, work is a real therapy. Worry about work can kill. But work that is enjoyed, conscientiously done, and makes a vital contribution to the life of mankind, is one of our greatest blessings. I am not afraid of work. I can lie down by it and sleep like a baby, or I can sit and watch it by the hour without fear. Work without worry, without undue hurry, work that is accomplishing something is a great boon. So work. Don't worry! One requirement for membership in the Coronary Club is to worry about everything, whether you can help it or not.

Guilt, in any form, is a definite cause of stress. We blame everything for our troubles, but most often the trouble lies within us. A doctor told me recently that most of his patients don't need his pills. They need to get themselves straightened out inside. A woman called me several years ago and said, "You . . . , I hate you!" After she had ranted out, I calmly replied, "You don't hate me. You hate yourself and you are taking it out on me." She broke down, and finally came to see me. Years ago, she had an affair with a married man that ended in an abortion. She had worried about it, and carried

a sense of guilt for years. It had tormented her to the breaking point. On that Sunday, I said something that brought
her feelings to the surface. She found God's forgiveness for
her wrong and got rid of her stress. A sense of guilt over
wrongs, over alienation from God, brings tension.

Long ago Isaiah said, "Thou wilt keep him in perfect peace,
whose mind is stayed on thee: because he trusteth in thee"
(26:3). And Jesus said "Ye must be born again" (John 3:7).
Another requirement for membership in the Coronary Club
is to carry your guilt around with you.

A false scale of values is a very common cause of stress. We
have lost sight of what really matters in life. We work all our
lives to accumulate money and things, and if that is all, our
reward is ulcers and nervous tension and anxiety. We Americans are thing-crazy.

Years ago, an American symphony toured Japan. When
the symphony arrived in one town, the members were amazed
to discover a battery of cash registers in place. When asked
about them, the Japanese replied, "We have heard that the
sound of the cash register is the sweetest music to American
ears."

I recently saw a sign that read, "Home for sale." You can't
buy a home. You can buy a house, and if you put the right
values in it, you can make it a home.

Each weekday, the men on the staff at First Methodist
Church go to a nearby dimestore for coffee. As I walk
through the store, with counters piled high with merchandise,
I say to myself, "Here is all this stuff that I don't want."

Education is a great thing. But unless education teaches
us what matters in life, what the real values are, it is worthless. One of the most pathetic things I have ever seen is a
woman who had a nervous breakdown because she was not
accepted into a particular women's club in the town to which
she had moved. One requirement for membership in the

Coronary Club is to believe deeply that things that don't matter do matter.

Still another frequently observed cause of stress is lack of faith or trust in Jesus Christ. Several years ago, I had to take off some time from work. I was tense, nervous, anxious, under considerable strain. I spent some time in the hospital in Atlanta, and each day, several times a day, the doctor would come to visit with me. He'd sit by the bed, hold my chart, and look at me, and at it. Sometimes he'd talk and sometimes he wouldn't. The times he wouldn't talk bothered me most. One day, out of the blue, he said, "You aren't a Christian, are you?" I was stunned, but I began to think. I'd been a Methodist minister for several years then. I remembered when I was converted in Chickamauga in a tent revival conducted by the Colliers. But he went on, "You don't believe the Bible, do you?" I was trying to get ready to answer that one. I recalled the nights at home when we read the Bible together, and I remembered how much it meant to me over the years. But he went on, "Do you know where it says in the Bible, 'They that wait upon the Lord shall renew their strength'? And do you know where it says, 'All things are possible, only believe'?" I knew them both and was about to tell him so. But without waiting, he blurted out, "If you were a Christian, and if you believed the Bible, you wouldn't be in the mess you are in here today." He turned and walked out.

I had some hard thinking to do. I'd been trying to run my own life, without much means of support from God or anybody else. I thought I could do it myself. I was converted again that day at the hands of a doctor. Of course, like a good Methodist, I have backslidden many times, but the lesson has stayed. A poet has said, "I fight alone, and win or sink, I want no one to make me free. I want no Jesus Christ to think that he could ever die for me." Still another requirement for membership in the Coronary Club is to go on thinking you can do it yourself.

Well, nevertheless many of us seem to have a hundred things to do each day. In today's world there seems to be little hope of avoiding everything that causes stress. But there are some positive steps that can help us handle the pressures more effectively.

(1.) Decide what is important, and get rid of the rest. A man made a speech. When he finished he worried everybody about it, asking, "Did I do it good?" Finally, one honest brother said, "You done it good, but it wasn't worth doin'." What really matters for you? What is important? What do you want to accomplish? No one but you can decide what is important. Viktor Frankl, in *Man's Search for Meaning* (Beacon Press) writes: "Everything can be taken from a man but one thing: the last of the human freedoms—to choose one's attitude in any given set of circumstances." The Bible is filled with the idea of personal choice: "Choose this day whom you will serve" (Josh. 24:15 RSV). "If any man would come after me . . ." (Matt. 16:24 RSV). You decide what matters for you. Get rid of the unimportant.

(2.) Learn to organize life. A woman had a Japanese helper. She taught him a slogan: "A place for everything, and everything in place." One day she came home, and the house was a mess, disarrayed, disordered. Stunned, she asked him to repeat the slogan. He said, "Everything every place." Make a schedule of the things you have decided are important, do them one at a time, until all are done. Sir William Osler, one of the greatest doctors who ever lived, talked about "day-tight compartments." Live a day at a time. Organize your day. Jesus prayed, "Give us this day our daily bread" (Matt. 6:11). Stop worrying about the hundred things, organize them on the basis of importance, and do them. "God grant me the serenity to accept the things I cannot change; the courage to change the things I can; and the wisdom to know the difference."

(3.) Learn moderation in all things. Much of our stress comes because we over-do. Learn moderation in eating, sleeping, exercise, everything. You thought you had me there, didn't you? You thought I'd say drinking too. The only way to handle that is don't. A survey of 3000 top executives recently showed that 710 of them were overweight, excessively, and that 450 of these were suffering serious heart disorders. A doctor told me that a 20 percent increase in weight reduces the chances for living a normal life span by 50 percent. Practice moderation in everything. This calls for some discipline, but remember Jesus: "Enter ye in at the strait gate: . . . strait is the gate, and narrow is the way, which leadeth unto life, and few there be that find it" (Matt. 7:13-14).

(4.) Learn to relax and be quiet sometime every day, the same time if possible. I have a friend who has made a lot of money who takes his break at ten, two, and four o'clock. He doesn't have a cocktail, coffee, or a soft drink. He spends ten minutes each time in prayer and Bible reading. He is a relaxed person. Tagore, a marvelous Indian poet, taught that we should "wash our souls in silence" every day. Thomas Carlyle suggested that "silence is the element in which great things fashion themselves." John Masefield called it, "the practice of the getting of tranquility." Job wrote, "Acquaint now thyself with him, and be at peace" (22:21). Learn to relax, sit loosely in the saddle of life. Someone has wisely said, "Let down, or blow up."

(5.) Undress your soul at night just as you do your body. I'm afraid to ask, but do you sleep in your clothes at night? Why not also undress your soul, shed worries and anxieties when you go home. A requirement for membership in the Coronary Club is to take the briefcase home on the evenings you do not work at the office. Two men were riding the bus home one night. One looked worried and anxious, the other was tranquil and at peace. The worried one asked his friend some questions about how he could be so calm with everything going on in the world. His friend replied, "I let God take the night shift!"

Don't continue with guilt over past wrongs. You don't need to. "If we confess our sins, he is faithful and just to forgive us our sins, and to cleanse us from all unrighteousness" (1 John 1:9). The longer I live the more convinced I am that this is the most important verse in the Bible. Unforgiven wrong, whatever it is, destroys. Get rid of soul conflicts and be at peace with God, yourself, and other people.

(6.) There must be a constant intake of power from without if we are to handle life's stresses and strains and not crack up. We cannot handle life alone. Secretary Stanton said to Abraham Lincoln when the War Between the States was at its height, "I don't see how it is you are so calm when everything is going wrong." Mr. Lincoln replied, "Well, it's like this, Stanton, when you feel you are only a pipe for omnipotence to sound through, you do not worry much."

During the trial of eleven communists in New York, Judge Harold Medina struggled hard to keep his composure, trying to refrain from saying anything that might cause a mistrial. Under badgering he came close to breaking down. He took frequent recesses to recoup his forces. After one of these he reported: "I asked God to take charge of things, and that his will be done. All I know is, that as I lay on that couch in the heat of the darkened room, some kind of new strength seemed to flow into my veins. After fifteen minutes I was refreshed and went back to carry on the business of my court."

The most beautiful offer in the world is from the lips of Jesus: "Come unto me, all ye that labour and are heavy laden, and I will give you rest. Take my yoke upon you, and learn of me; for I am meek and lowly in heart, and ye shall find rest unto your souls. For my yoke is easy, and my burden is light" (Matt. 11:28-30). Notice the kind of rest he offers—not inactivity, not release from all pressures. He knows we need the right kind of pressure and tension. So he invites us to take on a new pressure: his yoke. Strange way to find freedom? Not at all. His yoke is adapted to our true nature as sons and daughters of God, so it is easy and light, and it makes all other pressures easier to bear. He simply meant, "Team up with me. Together we can handle any pressure and use it creatively."

The Lord is my pace setter, I shall not rush;
He makes me stop and rest for quiet intervals.
He provides me with images of stillness which restore
   my serenity.
He leads me in the ways of efficiency through calmness
   of mind.
And His guidance is peace.

Even though I have a great many things to accomplish
   each day,
I will not fret; for His presence is here.
His timelessness, His all importance will keep me in
   balance.
He prepares refreshment and renewal in the midst of my
   activity.

By anointing my mind with His oils of tranquility my
   cup of joyous energy overflows.

Surely harmony and effectiveness shall be the fruits of
my hours.
For I shall walk in the pace of my Lord and dwell in His
house forever.

　　　　　—Toki Miyashina
　　　　　　　"The Twenty-third Psalm for Busy People"

5

Love Makes the World Go 'Round

In preparation for this chapter read 1 Corinthians 13.

Hold it! Don't turn that page! I can hear some of you realistic, down-to-earth people, having read the title of this chapter, saying that love isn't practical. "It's fine to talk about love and forgiveness in Sunday school and from the pulpit, but out in the working world where people struggle for mastery, love won't work. Period." A dentist married a pedicurist, and they fought tooth and toenail for the rest of their lives. So do we. We go on saying, "I'll get even if it's the last thing I do." And we laugh out loud when the preacher says we ought to love our enemies, our business associates, and forgive our competitors. "Hell, no! Don't love them. Beat them!" (And that's a direct quote.) We are amused when someone suggests that we forgive the people who gossip about us, or the person who ruins our home, or the business-man who gets the new account. Oh yes, I know: that clerk was uncivil to you, the repairman overcharged you, the real estate agent lied to you, your relatives imposed on you, the tramp stole your watch while you fixed him a sandwich, your girl friend married someone else, the boss gave the promotion you deserved to another, a careless driver banged the fender on your new Roadrunner then didn't have a dime's worth of insurance, your rich uncle died and left it all to some church, your political opponents told the truth about you, your mother-in-law doesn't understand you!

How practical these things are. I've heard them all, and to some of them I can say "Me, too!" Somehow people think a preacher doesn't have much sense and isn't quite human. He doesn't know what goes on. How can he talk about love since he lives in an ivory castle where real living doesn't take place?

I got a letter some time back that started, "You S.O.B. You think you know about hate. Let me tell you about real hatred. . . ." And he went on to describe some things he thought I wouldn't know about. He didn't say a thing I hadn't heard or experienced. I still say, "Love makes the world go 'round!"

On an evening several years ago, a young Korean exchange student at the University of Pennsylvania left his room to mail a letter. When he turned from the mailbox, he stepped into the arms of eleven leather-jacketed teenaged boys. Without a word of explanation they attacked him with blackjacks, lead pipes, shoes, and fists. When the police found him later, he was dead in the gutter where they left him. All Pennsylvania, indeed the whole nation, was outraged. The district attorney got permission to try the boys as adults to secure the death penalty. Then a letter came from the dead boy's parents in Pusan. Twenty other relatives, besides the boy's parents, signed the letter. It read in part:

Our family has met together and we have decided

to petition that the most generous treatment possible within the laws of your government be given to those who have committed this criminal action. . . . In order to give evidence of our sincere hope contained in this petition, we have decided to save money to start a fund to be used for the religious, educational, vocational, and social guidance of the boys when they are released. . . . We have dared express our hope with a spirit received from the gospel of our Saviour Jesus Christ who died for our sins.

"Unbelievable?" you say. "How can people be so loving and forgiving? I don't understand." Ah, my friend, that's the kind of love that makes the world go 'round.

One of the moving stories of the Second World War is that of Coventry in England. The heart of the lovely city is the Cathedral. Coventry was bombed again and again until the whole area was devastated by Nazi ferocity. The city has been rebuilt, and the heart of it is still the Cathedral. The chief street in the city is a mall where people can walk leisurely, without dodging cars and buses. The Cathedral has been built anew, but built to emphasize the needs of human beings. The forecourt of the new Cathedral is the nave of the old Cathedral. It is now planted in grass, outlined by the broken tracery of charred walls and windows. Where the high altar once stood, there is a pile of rocks, crowned by a cross made from charred wood from the roof. Behind the cross are the words, "Father, forgive!" And to put into action the words of love, the people of Coventry received sixteen young people from Germany who gave a year of their time to the rebuilding of this shrine of peace and love. What was once a symbol of hate and destruction has become a sign of love and forgiveness to the whole world.

These aren't easy days in which to live. Our human relationships are so tangled and twisted. Communication isn't easy. Tempers flare. Feelings are hurt, lives ruined. All of us have more troubles and problems than we can carry. There's not a one of us but can be more than he is if somehow we can learn the truth: love makes the world go 'round. The world grows smaller, but the things that separate us seem to get bigger. But add it all up, then take another look at the cross, and see the love of Jesus in the face of the worst people could do to him: they lied about him, arrested him on trumped-up charges, swore false testimony at his trial. They spit on him, beat him, mocked him with a purple robe and a crown of thorns, stripped him and then hung him up for flies and buzzards to destroy. In the last writhing moments of his life, he whispered, "Father, forgive them; for they know not what they do" (Luke 23:34). This is the kind of love that makes the world go 'round!

There is not a one of us but can be more than he is if he begins to practice in his routine daily experiences the thing Jesus pointed out as the first commandment, the highest virtue, the greatest summary of the law: love.

Georgia Harkness tells of a young teacher in a southern high school teaching the ethics of Jesus as part of a history course. The teacher asked his class to read Kirby Page's book, *The Personality of Jesus*. On the examination, he asked, "Did Jesus really intend for people to live according to the ideals he taught?" One paper summed it up: "Yes, perhaps, sometimes!" It is not asking the impossible to suggest that today we begin to practice love in all our relationships; love that is outgoing, concerned with other people, good will for every person. A man came to me after a recent Sunday service and said, "You sure are making it hard for me with this love business. I hate Richard Nixon." He could certainly find some sympathizers. Yet, true love can handle every situation.

When this kind of love comes to live in us, we become different persons, more than we ever dreamed we could be. Life just cannot move along at the same old pace when we are surrendered to the God of love, and when his love begins to grow in us. William Thackeray describes it in *The Virginians*. When a young man falls in love with a young woman, it is astonishing how fond he becomes of every person connected with the family. He ingratiates himself with the maids. He gets along with the butler. He takes an interest in the footman. (Obviously this book is mighty old: who has footmen, butlers, or even maids these days?) He runs errands for the daughters. He gives advice and lends money to the son in college. He pats little dogs which he would otherwise kick. He laughs at papa's stories, stories that would break him out in yawns if anyone else told them. He beats time when Fanny plays her piece on the piano. He smiles indulgently when Bobby spills coffee on his shirt. Yes, love makes the world go 'round. Changes take place when the love of God begins to live and grow in us.

One Sunday morning I went into the early service with some feelings of resentment and bitterness toward a man who had given me a hard time all week about some insignificant thing. When we came to the Lord's Prayer, I couldn't say, "Forgive us our trespasses as we forgive those who trespass against us." The service went badly. After it was over, I went to find the man, and we got our differences ironed out, and both spoke words of forgiveness and love. At the eleven o'clock service, I could really pray, "Forgive us . . . as we forgive." This thing works. I dare you to try it for one week!

Love helps us forgive all who have wronged us, and get right all the things that separate us from people. A classic example is that of Sergeant Jacob Deshazer, one of the Doolittle fliers. He spent years in a Japanese prison camp, where he was beaten, starved, violated, tortured. One day he wrote on a piece of paper the results of his thoughts. Among the words were these: "Know that all mankind is doomed to be perfect; that we must love one another; that no one can come to the Father except through the Son." "We decided," he wrote later, "that we had no hatred for our guards, vicious as they were. They were ignorant and mean, but we thought there was some good in them. The only way to develop that goodness was through Christian understanding, not by brutally mistreating them as they were doing us." Deshazer then said, "That made sense in a prison camp and it still does. So I am going to return to Japan as a missionary and spend the rest of my life there, teaching the importance of love among men." He did.

What I am saying is hard, isn't it? You've been thinking about the people you literally hate, those who bear grudges against you, those whose necks you'd cheerfully wring if you could do it legally. How do you love people like this, you ask? You can't. Notice I said *you* can't. Love is of God, and it comes to live in our hearts when our lives are surrendered to him, the God of love whom Jesus revealed! Love in the highest sense is above the human. We can't manufacture it! J. B. Phillips wrote in *Making Men Whole* (Word Books): "Unhappily in our day the Christian religion is all too often reduced to a performance to please an external God, when to the early Christians it was plainly the invasion of their lives by a new quality of life—nothing less than the life of God himself!" Love begins to grow in us when our lives have been invaded by the love of God. For me to tell you to love your enemies, and forgive those who hate you would be utterly foolish. *You* can't do it! But when God takes charge and his love begins to live in you, then you and God together can forgive anybody.

In an address some years ago, the Bishops of the Methodist

Church said: "What the world needs is new men, souls made ready for the battle at the altar, for men who would wage spiritual warfare must be equipped with the weapons of the spirit, chief of which is love." The end of the matter is this: find an altar, in your church, by your bed tonight, or out in the dark by a lake, or wherever you can, and make surrender of your life to God, along with all the hates and grudges and irritations. Simply say to him, "Lord, I can't take all this rotten mess of hate, and poison, and rancor that shrivels my soul. I'm tired of carrying all this stuff inside me. I can't get rid of it by myself. Forgive me, cleanse me, restore me, make me something new. Fill me with your love."

And now comes the hard part. What I have said so far may just be words. The test of it is in what you do when you have prayed that and get up off your knees: go find the person you hate, or who hates you, and say "I'm sorry. Let's be friends. Or at least, let's not hate any longer." You may not be able to go, but there's the telephone, or the United States mail. This is the proof of surrender to the love of God and the reception of that love.

The person to whom you apologize may not respond positively. You will have relieved your own soul and you will have done all you can do. You then can go in peace, and grow in grace. You can always pray that God's spirit will soften a hard heart and work the miracle of transformation in another. You can look for chances to express love in service and word, hoping against hope that a reconciliation may be effected. Don't ever quit praying, and believing, and trying.

If love should count you worthy, and should deign
One day to seek your door and be your guest,
Pause 'ere you draw the bolt and bid him rest,
If in your old content you would remain;

For not alone he enters; in his train
Are angels of the mist, the lonely quest,
Dreams of the unfulfilled and unpossessed,
And sorrow, and Life's immemorial pain.
He wakes desires you never may forget,
He shows you stars you never saw before,
He makes you share with him forevermore
The burden of the world's divine regret.
How wise you were to open not, and yet
How poor if you should turn him from the door!
      —S. R. LYSAGHT
        "The Penalty of Love"

6

When Sorrow Comes

In preparation for this chapter read Hebrews 12:11-13.

The hardest thing we have to face is the problem of sorrow, suffering, and pain. All of these in some form are the lot of all men. Death comes to loved ones, our minds are torn and tortured as we wrestle with life, our bodies know the wrack and hurt and misery. The good and bad suffer alike. All of us know devout, humble people whose bodies are in constant torture. I stood by a bedside recently talking with a fellow who has been sick for years. He is a good man and his mind often struggles with the problem. His wife works to support the family. "Why must I be sick all my life?" he asked. We know good people whose loved ones die before their time. I sat with a family whose beautiful six-year-old had just died. There was no bitterness, but a question, "Why?"

The problem of evil is no new problem. Job, years before Christ, reminds us that "man is born unto trouble as the sparks fly upward" (Job 5:7). It is a universal problem, confronting us daily. We cannot escape it in ourselves or close our eyes to it in others. Scientists tell us that the capacity for pain develops in the baby before the capacity for pleasure. Suffering is a universal problem, found in babies, grownups, rich and poor, all nationalities alike. It is the lot of the human race, a mark of humanity, to suffer and know sorrow. G. A. Studdert-Kennedy, British Chaplain in World War I, said any person undisturbed by the pain and suffering of others is himself suffering from either hardening of the heart or softening of the brain. Through the years of recorded history the question "Why?" has formed on the lips of all people as they have confronted death, sickness, and suffering.

The problem of evil and suffering is one that we cannot solve. People have sought answers in every conceivable way and place. There seems to be no sensible answer. Job sought it in his suffering. David sought it when his soul was torn over the death of his son Absalom. Paul wrestled with his thorn in the flesh. The philosophers have sought answers. Even Jesus on his cross asked, "My God, my God, why hast thou forsaken me?" (Mark 15:34).

There are many possible reasons for the problem. An obvious as well as necessary reason is the impartial operation of the laws of the universe which makes a cosmos out of what would be a chaos. Another factor that creates suffering is the interdependence of people. There are two hundred million of us in the United States and three billion in the world. None of us is an island. What I do affects you and what you do affects me. Our freedom of choice brings suffering too. God made us free to choose our own way and we may choose right and wrong, good and bad. Our ignorance is a definite factor in human suffering. There is much that we just do not know. We are not omniscient. Sin in the world brings suffering. Man, by his willful wrong, harms not just himself but all people, and God as well. You see, there are many possible explanations for sorrow and yet it is a problem that we cannot solve. It looms large in our lives. We cannot escape it, hide from it, explain it. Yet we cannot be satisfied to leave it alone. We stand in the face of it and want something that we don't have.

No words can ever express our debt to sorrow, pain, suffering. Many of the Psalms were written in sorrow. Paul wrote some of his finest letters in prison. Bedford jail produced *Pilgrim's Progress*. Dante was in exile when he wrote *Divine Comedy*. Tennyson, the greatest poet of the nineteenth century, wrote *In Memoriam* after the death of his friend Hallam. Sorrow made Paderewski a master musician. Suffering made Spurgeon a great preacher. The Book of Acts was written in persecution as was Revelation. Beethoven wrote most of his matchless symphonies after he was deaf. Nathaniel Hawthorne lost his job as a custom house clerk and turned to writing, producing among other things *The Scarlet Letter*. In our personal lives we often owe new insights and truths to suffering. It may develop a courage, a sympathy never before known. The whole race of men owes a debt to sorrow and pain.

The problem of suffering is with us all and always. Our chief concern should not be why we suffer, for we have seen that there seems to be no sensible answer. Our chief concern should be with how to suffer, bear sorrow, know pain. You can be more than you are if you can learn to handle these things. There are a number of ways of responding to the reality of evil in our lives. Here are three possibilities.

(1.) We can be rebellious. All of us feel that way at times. Only emotionally sick people enjoy poor physical health, or sorrow, or suffering in any form. All of us feel rebellious at the pain and hurt in our lives and around us. I got a letter from a mother whose son had been killed in service. In it she said, "I never intend to put my foot in a church again. The church has lied to me. It has fooled me into believing what isn't so. I have been taught that if you pray you'll get an answer. I prayed that my boy would come home safely. He's dead. I hate God. You can't trust him!"

I stood by the bed of a man stricken with an incurable disease. He said, "There is no God. There couldn't be. I have a wife and two children to care for. Why should I suffer and cause them suffering?" We can be and often are terribly furious with "fate," if you want to call it that, for allowing these things to happen. Being rebellious isn't the answer.

Almost every week someone says, "My mother died this week," or "Our son left home and we don't know where he is," or "I lost my job this week." Occasionally one of them will say, "This religion stuff is no good, or this would not happen to me. I've been in church regularly, paid my pledge. Now this. I'm through with church." Bitterness does not help. It only increases the problem. It alienates friends. Makes us unfit to live with. Takes away peace of mind. The person who kicks against the goads only harms himself and breaks his foot.

(2.) A second and better way of handling sorrow and suffering is to make the best of it.

> For every ailment under the sun,
> There is a remedy or there is none;
> If there be one, try to find it;
> If there be none, then never mind it.
> —*Pulpit Preaching*

To the everlasting credit of mankind, more often than not, the response to suffering is, "What can't be cured must be endured." Our smiling neighbors have secret hurts and sorrows. There are plenty of people with physical and mental ailments who never let on to their friends and family. There are those who suffer family problems and misunderstandings who never give way to the agony they suffer. You can make the best of it. This is better than rebellion. You can roll with the punches, take it on the chin, keep a stiff upper lip.

(3.) But there is an even better way to handle pain, suffering, and sorrow when they come: use them creatively. It is possible to do that. One can take the long view of these things and make them serve one's spiritual well-being. This is the Christian's way of handling them. The present suffering seems bad and unbearable, but Christians realize that it can be used, transformed into joy, peace of mind, usefulness for others. The Danish philosopher Kierkegaard wrote a book entitled *The Gospel of Suffering.* Job said it: "When he hath tried me, I shall come forth as gold" (Job 23:10).

I went to visit a steel mill recently. The furnaces are heated to great intensity. The crude ore is placed in a crucible where a transformation takes place. Then the pure ore is separated from the dross. When this process is complete, the impurity, the slag is taken off and the pure ore pours forth in a stream of fire. This happens to gold also and to other metals. Without undergoing such intense heat, no pure metal would be available.

It is fair to compare this process with suffering and sorrow. Each of us can become more than we are as a result of the testing of our souls. In fact, we do not understand the sorrows of others until we have known sorrow ourselves. The best things in life are hardest to get. Unless the rose is crushed there is no perfume. The sandalwood tree scents the axe that cuts it.

Someone said of Phillips Brooks, "He might have saved himself and so prolonged his life. Others do, but he was always giving, giving himself to any who needed him." To which another replied, "Yes indeed, he might have saved himself but in doing so, he would not have been Phillips Brooks."

Often out of sorrow there comes great character. A woman had just been to the doctor. When told that she had cancer and could live only a short while, she cried out, "I wish I had never been made." A friend said to her, "You have not been made. You are being made now."

The word *tribulation* is suggestive. It came from the Latin word *tribulum* which was the tool made of a block of wood with iron teeth driven into it and used to separate wheat and chaff. Likewise suffering and sorrow, when rightly used, may carry out the same function in our lives.

In the Book of Revelation the question is asked, "What are these which are arrayed in white robes? and whence came they?" The answer is given: "These are they which came out of great tribulation, and have washed their robes, and made them white in the blood of the Lamb" (Rev. 7:13-14).

I read about a man who saw a butterfly struggling to come out of its cocoon. He watched it struggle intensely. The man, thinking he would help, took his knife and cut the end of the cocoon to let it out. The butterfly then emerged easily, but it could not fly. The struggle, though a somewhat painful experience, was a necessary and vital part of the creature's development.

Suffering may lead us into closer fellowship with God. It may lead to sweet relationships with people. Suffering, sorrow, pain may be the means to larger usefulness. There is no gospel in mere suffering. But if suffering leads us into larger sympathies with God's children, and into larger living, then it becomes good news. It was said of Jesus that he learned obedience by the things he suffered. He endured pain not just for himself but for others.

Tennyson struggled with the sufferings of doubt and despair. Finally he won through and gave to mankind these words:

> Strong Son of God, immortal Love,
>   Whom we, that have not seen thy face,
>   By faith, and faith alone, embrace,
> Believing where we cannot prove.
>
> —*In Memoriam*

I read the deeply moving story of a child who was cruelly malformed at birth. The decision of life or death for the child at that moment lay with the attending physician. Should such a child be permitted to live and enter a world of life-long pain and terrible handicap, or perhaps better, should it be delivered from it all before it knew? All the physician needed to do in this case was to do nothing. But he was a conscientious physician, and a Christian. He did everything he could and the child lived. For a long time he blamed himself bitterly for bringing her into the world a helpless cripple. Years went by and he lost trace of her completely, and had partly forgotten her. One night he sat in a great hall and listened to a concert of Christmas music. A girl played carols on the harp. She was terribly crippled, but nobody gave it any thought. She played so beautifully that everybody was deeply moved and listened transfixed in holy silence. When the concert was ended, the physician went down to find out who the girl was. It was then that her mother told him. He threw his arms around her and drew her close to himself. "My child! There has been a heavy burden on my heart all these years, and tonight you have lifted it. Take your harp and play it again. I want to listen to it alone. 'Silent Night, Holy Night'." The two sat by themselves in the great hall after all the others had gone. Not a word was spoken. The soft deep notes of the harp seemed to dissolve all the heavy mists of mystery. Every burden was gone.

And you too, my friend, called upon to bear some sorrow, some pain, some suffering, may be able to turn them to greater usefulness.

God suffers with us. He not only suffers with us, he gives us strength to bear and use our suffering. Paul said: "Who shall separate us from the love of Christ?" (Rom. 8:35). And he concluded that nothing in this world can separate us from him.

Laurence Housman wrote a poem he called "A Prayer for the Healing of the Wounds of Christ." The last two lines are beautiful to me:

> Also, for all things perishing, he saith,
> My grief, my pain, my death.

In our sorrow, pain, and grief God says, "My sorrow, my pain, my grief." It makes a difference to know that God looks with compassion into the eyes of an afflicted child, or with love into an open grave, or with tenderness into the face of suffering parents. God understands and we do not bear any pain or sorrow or suffering alone.

In Lytton Strachey's *Eminent Victorians* (Putnam) is a fine statement about General Gordon: "The Sunday before General Gordon started for the Sudan, he drove around London to a number of churches to take communion as many times as possible, 'In order,' he said, 'to start thus brim full of God.' " This is the secret of bearing suffering, accepting it, using it creatively. Apart from God there is no answer to the why or the how of suffering.

Cyrus Albertson tells of a violin maker who searched all his life for wood that would make violins with a certain haunting sound of beauty. At last he found what he wanted in wood cut right at the timberline on a high mountain. Timberline in the Rockies is the last strand of trees, often twelve thousand feet above sea level. Up there winds blow so fiercely that even bark has no chance to grow on the windward side. All the branches point in one way. A tree must stay on its knees to live at all. But the wood in these trees is found to be the most resonant in the world. It makes wonderful violins and they in turn make music to stir men's souls. But these trees live on their knees. So must we. You who suffer, through your experience, can be turned to joy, usefulness, and beauty of character, if you trust God and love him with all your heart. In his power suffering can be transformed, and you can become much more than you are.

Perhaps you have not yet known any suffering and sorrow. You will. The best preparation you can make is to give your life, soul, body, and mind in love and surrender to him of whom Paul said, "If God be for us, who can be against us?" (Rom. 8:31b).

7

Making the Most of What You Have

In preparation for this chapter read Matthew 25:14-30.

How to make the very most of what you have is one of life's insistent matters. Our Lord told a story about it. "A man going on a journey called his servants and entrusted to them his property; to one he gave five talents [pieces of money], to another two, to another one, to each according to his ability. Then he went away." These three men looked around them for ways of handling the money entrusted to their care.

The one who had received five talents, about five thousand dollars, was a bright and resourceful fellow. He studied the weather, listened to reports of drought in Syria, studied the possibilities of good crops, got acquainted with the leading men in the caravans passing through his section from Damascus. He made shrewd judgments on the possibilities of war and peace. He noted the change in prices of goods. He invested his master's money and doubled it.

The man with two talents was more of a plodder than the

first, and he believed in hard work. So he worked from dawn to dark, working a double shift, moonlighting, doing anything he could to make money for his master. He worked so hard that he also doubled his master's money.

The third man did neither. He had no ideas about making money for his master. He had no imagination, no discipline, so he just hid the money in the ground.

When the master returned, he commended the faithful servants who had doubled the money given to them. He sternly rebuked the servant who had hidden the money in the ground. He must have shouted, "Take the talent from him, and give it to him who has ten talents!" The man lost the talent he had.

Jesus told this story for the benefit of the one-talent man. We use talent and ability to mean the same thing. The one-talent man stands front and center. There aren't many five- or even two-talent people. Not many Edisons, Curies, Lincolns, Shakespeares, Livingstones. But how many one-talent, ordinary people there are. The good Lord must have loved them; he made so many of them.

Peculiar dangers confront the ordinary person. He is tempted by the devil to say, "With my poor equipment, nothing is expected of me. What can I do? I'm afraid to take a chance. Suppose I try and fail?" Oddly enough, the one-talent man is prone to resent the two- and five-talent men. He resents those better endowed, holds a grudge against life itself. He blames God for not doing a better job by him. He accuses God of expecting something for nothing. Often the world's ills can be traced to the ordinary man, who says, "What do I matter? I'm just one, and I don't count."

This parable reminds us that each is endowed with a gift. There's no silly doctrine of equality or uniformity or average. The same five-two-one applies to us. But God expects us to use what we have and our reward is in keeping, not with what we have, but what we do with what we have. There is no way of estimating the importance of the ordinary man, especially when he falls into the hands of a mighty God.

Shakespeare could never have been known outside his own province had it not been for the printer and the bookbinder and the keeper of the glue pots. Many people say, "I'm just one note on the piano of life." But suppose that note goes sour. The whole harmony is ruined. The ordinary people allowed Hitler to overrun Germany. Ordinary people put up with inequalities, wrongdoing in government by saying my vote doesn't matter. Three presidents have been selected by one vote. Charlotte Brontë said it is "better to try all things and find all empty than to try nothing and find your life a blank." This is making the very most of your life, whatever it is. You can be more than you are. You are important!

How do we make the very most of our lives? How do we take whatever gift God has granted us and use it to be more than we are? Look at six words.

(1.) *Examination.* Take stock of your life. Take a good solid look at your abilities. One, two, or five? Probably ordinary. Nothing unusual about you. What abilities do you possess? What are your strong points? You may have several which can be developed into a satisfying life. You may have only one. But one or several, the world's greatest resources lie under your hat and stand on your feet. If you can't be a star, be a supporter. If you can't have the lead role, then be in the supporting role; it's just as important. See what you have, what abilities, and use these.

Kenneth Hilderbrand tells of one of the men who went with Richard E. Byrd to the North Pole. He fell in love with the North and wanted to go back. But there were no expeditions for the North, and so he had to settle down to unconventional work. He became an unhappy man because he could not fulfill his heart's desire. Instead of dreaming of explorations to the North, he might have explored his own neighborhood for boys who needed help, and organized them into Boy Scout troops, or Boys' Clubs. He could have fired in them admiration for bravery and teamplay and other qualities needed for an expanding life. Since he couldn't do all he wanted, he was unwilling to do anything. Take stock of your abilities. What have you got? Be honest about it. "Know thyself," said Socrates. This is the beginning of being more than you are!

(2.) *Discipline* your abilities. Everytime someone gets a promotion, we make a major discovery: "He's lucky." "He gets the breaks." "Everything is in his favor." Luck has little to do with it in most cases. Luck is usually found at the exact point where preparation meets opportunity. More people go ahead by push than by pull. Someone has reminded us that success is not so much due to the favorable arrangement of the stars at our birth as to the steady trail of sparks from the grindstone of hard work each day.

I remember "Babe" Zaharias. She was an international sensation the year the Olympics were in Los Angeles. She placed first in javelin, eighty-meter hurdles, and second in high jump. Then she turned to golf. When she won the National Women's Amateur and British Women's Amateur, people said it was inevitable—she is an automatic champion. When "Babe" took up golf she found a good instructor, learned all he had to teach her. Then she practiced, sometimes twelve hours a day. She would hit as many as a thousand golf balls in an afternoon. Sometimes she would swing until her hands were sore. Then she'd stop, tape her hands and go right back. Is that automatic? She later showed the same courage in her bout with cancer.

Discipline is a word we hate. That accounts for so much of the restlessness, so much crime, and so much of the rottenness in government, industry, religion, education and everywhere else. When you have discovered your abilities, or ability, then discipline it. You will become more than you are!

(3.) *Motivation.* "Babe" Zaharias *wanted* to play golf. The great contributors to life are the strongly motivated people: they want to do something. The aimless ones drift to and fro, never caring whether the store keeps or not. They never know joy or fulfillment. They aren't mean, just shallow. Not wicked, just empty. They have no means or purpose in life. The one-talent man is like a boy who said, "I don't want to be great; I only want to be comfortable." Comfortable conformity is ruining us.

A teen-ager was in the bathroom one morning, crying. Her father, impatient to get in to shave, asked what the problem was. She snubbed, "I can't get my hair to do right!" He asked what she was trying to do to it, and after she explained, the father made a bargain. "If you will comb it straight back, part it in the middle and tie a ribbon on the end and wear it a week, I'll give you twenty dollars." Now you know and I know that a teen-ager will do a lot for twenty dollars. She agreed. Friday came and she came to collect the money. After dad had paid off, he asked, "How did it go this week?" She replied, "Well, on Monday, when I first went to school I would just as soon have gone in my nightgown as with my hair combed like that. But daddy, a funny thing has happened this week. Today, every girl in my class came to school with her hair combed straight back, parted in the middle, with a bow on the end!"

To succeed in life, there must be the motivation. King Edward VII of England asked William Booth how he could give himself to such hard and thankless work with the poor and ignorant and wicked of London. Booth replied: "Some men's passion is gold, some men's passion is fame, my passion

is souls." The passion to do, the "want to" is absolutely es-
sential. The "want to" will make you more than you are!

(4.) *Enthusiasm.* Put it to work. The one-talent man was
not condemned because he used his talent for evil. He didn't
use it at all. He was not condemned because he failed to gain
other talents. He was condemned because he didn't even try.
Very often people with one talent achieve more than five-
talent people when they use what they have. There is a story
from the gold rush days of a man named Jim who remained
a ne'er-do-well in the midst of riches. Jim had the gold fever,
but he didn't have the digging principle. Matthew Arnold
wrote, "Genius is mainly an affair of energy." Benjamin
Franklin said, ". . . plough deep while sluggards sleep."

A boy was boarding a bus to seek his fortune. "Now
Michael, me boy," said his aged Irish uncle, "just remember
the three bones and you'll get along all right." A curious
bystander asked what were the three bones. "Sure, now,"
replied the aged Irishman, "and wouldn't it be the wishbone,
the jawbone, and the backbone. It's the wishbone that keeps
you going after things. It's the jawbone that keeps you asking
the right questions. It's the backbone that keeps you at it till
you find it." How true.

There is no substitute for hard, enthusiastic work with
whatever ability you may have. Many a man has taken a
single talent and made his mark in the world by working at
that one thing. This gives vitality to ability. The word
enthusiasm means "god-possessed." It means to approach
work eagerly, warmly, fervently. If you do, you can be more
than you are!

(5.) *Imagination.* Someone has said, "The derelict will
remain a derelict until a vision of a higher self grips him."
Why is it that we can all walk the same streets, see the same
things, live in the same world, and suddenly someone else
gets hold of something anyone with one eye and half sense

could have seen? "Why didn't I think of that?" Some of the most illustrious people were regarded as dull in childhood. Edison was called "an addled boy." Winston Churchill could never pass his exams. Isaac Newton was at the bottom of his class. A poet has written:

> Two men looked out of prison bars;
> One saw mud, the other stars.

A lot of people have dozed by the fire listening to a singing water kettle, but James Watts saw a steam engine. He said when his invention was completed: "You see it working for the first time. I saw it working long ago in my mind's eye." A sculptor sees not just a block of stone, but a statue. An artist sees not canvas but a painting of rare beauty. What ideal have you for yourself? What do you see in yourself? What goal is set? Imagination is desperately important to using what you have to the fullest. Never lose your sense of awe and wonder and inquisitiveness. You can be more than you are.

(6.) *Aspiration.* The ordinary abilities of our lives are vastly increased when they are yielded to the mastery of Jesus Christ. When he has his way in our lives, there is a greater power than any of us ever realize any other way. When his spirit guides us, our life takes on a meaning that it cannot have otherwise.

Take the disciple Peter, for example. He was a fisherman and I suspect resigned to the fact that he would always be one. Jesus came along and lifted his sights. He called this man "Simon" and then said, "Thou art Peter. . . ." He was saying, "Simon is your name, but there is more to you than even you dream about. So I'll build my church on the kind of faith and stuff you have." This is a clear example of what Jesus does in our lives.

Get all the education you can; explore the natural world with the scientists; learn to be at home with all kinds of people; make a success in business too; do what society demands of you; develop your skills. But even in doing all that, you will fall short of that greatness, splendor, power that could be yours if you surrender your life to Jesus Christ. You may be a good doctor, a good citizen, a mighty lawyer, or an outstanding scientist, but you can be an even greater one if you are possessed by the spirit of Jesus Christ. You may be a good parent, a fine homemaker, but in these too your life will be enhanced if you are possessed by Jesus Christ. He brings out the very best in us. Someone said of a friend, "I love you not only for what you are, but for what I am when I am with you." Jesus makes us something when we are with him.

People who know arctic waters are fascinated by icebergs. Often one will be sighted moving against the wind, shimmering majestically in the sun. Surface ice floats with the current. The iceberg, nine-tenths under water, flows with a deeper current and is borne against surface opposition. Dwell deep, my soul; dwell deep in Jesus, and you can move against all surface opposition.

Dr. Edward L. R. Elson, pastor of the National Presbyterian Church, Washington, D.C., tells some interesting things about the late President Dwight Eisenhower. This man was keenly aware of his need for a constant source of help and inspiration, and Dr. Elson tells of seeing him in the congregation on Sunday, singing with the other worshipers:

> Are we weak and heavy laden
> Cumbered with a load of care,
> Precious Saviour still our refuge:
> Take it to the Lord in prayer.
> —Joseph Scriven

He carried the heaviest load of any man in the nation. He went to the right source for help.

One Easter just before our sunrise service in the Atlanta Stadium, I was talking with Francis Tarkenton. He said, "I never pray to win a game. As a quarterback I pray for strength to lead my team well, to do my very best, to have calm presence of mind." Later he said, "Jesus promised strength for living. When I am playing a game, I know that all my strength and wisdom come from him. He gave me talent to play and I want to use it not only to play football, but to bring more people to Christ." He became more than he was through Christ. So can you!

You and I are searching, young and old, for something to give reality to life. Long ago a man said, "I am the way . . ." (John 14:6). He was Jesus Christ. "I am come . . ." said he, "that they might have life, and that they might have it more abundantly" (John 10:10). He meant that. And when people, young or old, let Jesus come alive in them, life takes on meaning.

Felipe Alou tells that in his room in Whitcomb Hotel in San Francisco he sat reading Romans 10:13: "For whosoever shall call upon the name of the Lord shall be saved." The light dawned. Felipe became a Christian and has become an international figure. He has found life with a capital *L*. How about you? Here's how to make the very most of what you have! Here's how to be more than you are!

8

Take
a Little Honey

In preparation for this chapter read Psalm 103.

Way back in the dim beginnings of recorded history, a gruff old Israelite named Jacob sent his sons into a strange country to get grain. They were faced with famine, and this was the second time these men had gone for help. The first venture brought sadness to father Jacob, for the business manager of Egypt had kept his youngest son as hostage. Old Jacob could not know that the man in charge of grain in Egypt was also his son, Joseph, whom his jealous brothers had sold into slavery years before. As his sons prepared to leave, the old man helped them get their things together, and made up gifts for the authorities in Egypt. Among other things, he said, "Take a little honey!" I know he was talking about the fruit of the hive, but that statement has a deep spiritual meaning for me, and I have discovered that this is a great way to live. In fact, by doing this, you can be more than you are.

Centuries passed. One night Jesus was at dinner with some friends. A woman burst into the house from the streets, and without warning broke a box of expensive ointment on Jesus' head. The disciples grumbled about it, insisting that it was a waste and might have been used to buy food for the poor. But Jesus saw it differently. She brought her admiration to him while he lived, and he treasured it so highly that he said that wherever his gospel should be preached, this would be remembered as her memorial. Nineteen hundred years later we are still talking about it.

A few more centuries went by and one night as I was driving a lonely backroad across middle Georgia, I had car trouble. I couldn't fix it, and cars came through that way very infrequently. The only moving thing I saw for two hours was a twinkling star a million miles away. Miles from nowhere, I was dejected. Later, a transport truck pulled up and stopped and the driver got out and gave me a hand. He helped me get into the next little town where I could telephone home. As he left I asked him why he stopped. I knew it was against company policy. He said that years before he and his family moved to a little town in North Carolina. The house they had bought wasn't ready. The local Methodist preacher let them live with him until the house was ready. He vowed then and there that he'd help anyone he could in need, and especially Methodist preachers. To that time we had not told each other who we were, and when I told him I was a Methodist minister, I thought he would go into orbit! His one comment was, "I have paid a debt on a lonely country road."

This is a simple message: "Take a little honey!" There is so much sadness and heartache in the world, so much hatred, so much mistrust. We live in such a hurry. We crowd the days with so many things. The problems are so big and seem so impossible of solution. Every person I know has a grief, a sorrow, an unsatisfied longing. There's not a one of us but wants to be more than he is. We can be. Gipsy Smith preached one day on Park Avenue in New York. After the service, a woman, obviously well off, said to him, "Mr. Smith, never forget, in every congregation there is some heart that's breaking."

Charles Malik, Christian statesman from Lebanon, once said: "The problems of the world are prodigious in size to be sure. They seem insoluble. But there isn't a single one of them that will not yield to solution, provided we take our stand on the basis of Christian principles."

One of these basic Christian principles is love and concern and kindness for our fellow human beings as we go along life's way. The Bible is a great book. If we'd read it, we'd get along a lot better, and we could be more than we are. It reports the wisdom of God and man over the ages, and it is the universal opinion of the Bible that kindness is better than coldness, love than hate, trust than jealousy. Paul wrote, "Be kindly affectioned one to another" (Rom. 12:10). The writer of Proverbs put it bluntly when he said, "A soft answer turneth away wrath, but grievous words stir up anger" (Prov. 15:1). There is not a lock on earth so rusty but that the key of love will open it.

Plenty of people go into life with native ability, education, and then fail. They fail because they have not learned this fundamental lesson of kindness. Push! Shove! Grab! In business we are all business. In church we can be so unkind. In social activities we gossip and are cruel. Big cities get cold and impersonal. Hurry! Run! Scramble!

Ella Wheeler Wilcox was close to a universal truth when she wrote:

> So many gods, so many creeds,
> So many paths that wind and wind,

When all this old world needs,
Is just the art of being kind!
                    —"The World's Need"

Maybe this isn't all the world needs, but kindness would take us a long way in the direction of solving some of life's knotty problems.

We take each other so for granted! Norman Cousins, editor of the *Saturday Review/World* once said, "Impersonality has become an epidemic." We take for granted the little, simple daily acts of kindness that people do for us. They go unnoticed. We fail to take advantage of opportunities to do simple little acts of kindness for other people. It really isn't difficult to say thank you and please, but these words have slipped from our vocabularies to a large degree. Things are so impersonal. A woman dialed a number recently, and a voice on the other end said, "Hello. This is a person speaking. Our automatic answering device is out being repaired." People stop being people and become cogs and wheels and numbers. They are hands in a factory, patients in a doctor's office, depositors in a bank, members of a congregation. We have taken the John Smithness out of John Smith.

Some time ago, I asked to see the president of a large retail store in Atlanta. When we had exchanged pleasantries, he startled me with the question, "Well, what is your complaint?" I said, "I have no complaint. I think you are doing a great job for a lot of people in our city, and I just wanted to thank you." He nearly fainted. He and I had worked together on the Metropolitan Boy Scout Executive Committee and I just wanted to thank him for what he was doing. Obviously, he wasn't accustomed to such treatment.

A woman got on a bus in Atlanta recently. A man got up and gave her his seat. She fainted. When she came to, she thanked him, and he fainted.

I got on the elevator one day in one of those old-fashioned buildings that still use operators. It was crowded. Tempers were on edge. Someone had missed a floor and was berating the operator. When I stepped off at my floor, I turned and deliberately thanked the operator for getting me where I wanted to go. Her face lighted up like a Christmas tree.

Years ago, on our first appointment, there was a Sunday school teacher in the adult division who did an outstanding job. I listened to her very often. One day I wrote her a note of thanks. A few days later there was an expensive book on my desk with this sad note: "I have been teaching for many years. You are the first person ever to write me a note of thanks. You'll never know what it meant to me."

I'm not pleading for some superficial, social veneer or pretty finesse. I'm asking something far more important, something for which human souls are starved: let's stop taking people for granted and accept them as persons and show gratitude for what they are and for what they do. That grocery clerk was snippy? Who knows what may be going on in his mind, perhaps his wife is sick, or a child has failed. Milkman, bus driver, laundryman, repairman—these are people, people for whom Christ died, people with needs and problems just like yours and mine. Gary Moore used to close his television show by saying, "Be very kind to each other out there."

There are people all around us who are discouraged with themselves and with life generally and who need encouragement to go on. A young man climbed up on the railing of a bridge, about to take his own life. A policeman caught his coattail and pulled him down. After some discussion, the policeman made a bargain: the boy would tell everything he could think of that was bad about the world. Then the policeman would tell everything that was good. If, when they had finished, the boy still wanted to jump, he could. So the boy recited all his woes, everything that he thought was wrong with the world. When he had finished, boy and policeman locked arms and both jumped into the river. Have you ever been there, feeling so low, so down and out that it was all you could do to keep from taking that overdose, or putting the gun to your temple, or going to the river? Someone asked Charles Kingsley one day about the secret of his happy life. He answered, "I had a friend."

The woman I described in the beginning came to Jesus with a need of her own. She was a woman of the streets. She had seen Jesus at work. She had heard him speak the forgiving word, do the kind deed. So she came, bringing her box of ointment to bless him for what he had done for others. But she had a need. She may have said, "I'm soiled and dirty. Maybe he can cleanse me." He did. Others found fault with her. He spoke the redeeming word she needed to hear. It was probably the first kind word she had heard about herself since she was some mother's baby. She came in as a streetwalker, and left to walk the streets to heaven. She may have been Mary Magdalene who went to the cross with Jesus' mother. Here is one of Jesus' marks of greatness. He could see beneath the veneer, the sham, and see what people could become. Maybe you have been there. Life looked bleak and dismal, then someone came with a word that lifted and healed. James Whitcomb Riley wrote in "Let Something Good Be Said":

> Forget not that no fellow being yet
> May fall so low but love may lift his head,
> Even the cheek of shame with tears is red,
> So let something good be said!

There are the sick and the aged. How useless and helpless many of them feel. As people get older, they get the feeling that they don't amount to much, aren't wanted or needed.

Ministers have all kinds of experiences: sad, happy, depressing, uplifting. One of the saddest of my ministry had to do with an old man who lived in a convalescent home. His wife had been cruel to him, and the children had scorned him. Finally, his wife died, and the children put him in this convalescent home. They thought they were rid of him. They didn't go near, and never wrote or called. He was pathetic. I'd go as often as I could and read to him, and pray with him, and take him some little gift. When I'd miss a week or so, he'd call and plead with me to come. When we took Holy Communion to the shut-ins, I'd always take it to him. He was so appreciative. Finally, he died. His was one of the biggest funerals I ever conducted. Flowers banked the chapel, sons and daughters and grandchildren came and wept copiously, and one of them very appropriately fainted. As I stood to read about many mansions, and looked into the faces of these people, I cried too. I remembered a lot of lonely days of heartbreak, dark nights when he would have loved a flower, a card, or a visit. Thank goodness, he didn't leave them a dime. He left it to the church and to charity. We in the churches have a great opportunity to put our profession into practice. I go into the hospitals nearly every day as does every other pastor. We see what a little kindness means to people who are sick, or in a convalescent home, or shut-in at home. If you are too busy to be kind, you are just too busy.

Why be kind? Why go out of my way to help anyone? Why bother with taking a little honey? Several reasons. God has been kind to us. James wrote in his letter, "Every good gift and every perfect gift is from above, and cometh down from the Father of lights, with whom is no variableness, neither shadow of turning" (James 1:17). And centuries before Isaiah said it beautifully: "Thou wilt keep him in perfect peace, whose mind is stayed on thee: because he trusteth in thee" (Isa. 26:3).

A woman went to a photographer for a portrait. She got herself all prettied up, and then said to the artist, "I want you to do me justice." He looked at her carefully, and then replied, "Lady, what you need is not justice, but mercy." How much mercy we have received from God.

Why take a little honey? All of us are made in the image of God and we ought to treat each other as sacred beings. Bishop Gerald Kennedy once told of a colony in Westphalia, Germany, dedicated to the treatment of epileptics and mentally deficient people. A very wealthy man was being shown through. They brought him to the children's ward. What he saw moved him deeply. He asked his guide how many of these children could be helped to live normal, or nearly normal lives. The guide replied, "One in a hundred." The wealthy man thought a moment, and then said, "It isn't worth it." The guide said quietly, "Suppose that one were your son?" You see, each of us is made in the image of God. He loves us each as if he did not have another in all the world to love.

Why take a little honey? There's enough trouble in the world without my adding anything to it. Ian Maclaren used to say, "Let us be kind to one another, for most of us are fighting a hard battle." And another has said, "When you help a neighbor up the hill you get to the top yourself."

Why take a little honey? The practice of kindness works miracles in our lives. A woman who had been active in the church for twenty years one day asked me, "Do you remember the wretched health I had when you first came to this church? Do you remember what a nervous wreck I was?" I remembered. Then she said, "I have had so many burdens to bear in my family, that today I am a relatively well woman." Carrying the loads of other people makes our own lighter. To help another is to help ourselves.

Why take a little honey? It works miracles in the lives of

those on whom kindness is practiced. There is not a person alive who will not respond to kindness. Julia Carney was right when she wrote:

> Little deeds of kindness, little words of love,
> Help to make earth happy, like to heaven above!
> —"Little Things"

One final question: Where do we get the ability to show kindness now, to take a little honey into all of living? This is not a virtue put on like paint on the house. Love comes to live in us when we surrender to him who is love. When his love fills our lives, then we are motivated by tenderness and compassion. The New Testament pictures Jesus as being kind, thoughtful, considerate, helpful, hopeful. We become like those with whom we associate. When we live close to Jesus we become like him.

9

The Fine Art of
Stopping and Starting

In preparation for this chapter read Philippians 4.

Is there anyone who does not have a habit he would like to break? Almost every person has some habit that keeps him from achieving wholeness or real happiness. It may be an overt habit like drinking, or profanity, or gambling. It may be a more subtle thing like self-pity, or being overly critical, or jealousy, or worry, or impure thoughts, or greed. We have been quick to condemn the sins of the flesh, but slow to recognize the destructiveness of attitudes, and the more subtle sins of the spirit. But many a habit unseen by the world gets hold upon us and threatens our security, our peace, and our very existence as persons. Jesus pointed out the wrongness of murder, but he also emphasized the wrongness of hate. Attitudes were mighty important to him. We spend the first half of our lives learning habits that shorten the other half.

Rarely a day passes but that someone asks me, "How do you break a bad habit and begin a good one?" Habits can be changed. Bishop Edwin Holt Hughes used to say of smoking, "I know a man can quit smoking. I've done it six times myself."

Our habits determine our happiness ultimately. Someone has rightly said, "A mature personality has acquired the habits and skills which can sustain happiness." We do not gather grapes from thorns, nor do we gather figs from thistles. Happiness cannot be had from a life cluttered with habits which bemean or destroy us. We can't find genuine happiness in life until we create the personal qualities that merit it. These qualities do not come to us automatically. They are acquired over the years by discipline, by training, by effort.

The story of Daniel is an intriguing one. It is about a man whose habits, acquired over the years, brought him the ultimate happiness: the ability and the willingness to stand before the severest temptation and not waver. Nebuchadnezzar laid siege to Jerusalem and captured it. He took some captives home with him. Among them were Daniel, Shadrack, Meshach, and Abednego. He ordered a special food for these men to make them fit for the king's service. "But Daniel purposed in his heart that he would not defile himself . . ." (Dan. 1:8). He had formed the habit of simplicity in eating and drinking. He refused to be swayed.

Later, the king made an image of gold and ordered all people to come together and at a given signal fall down and worship the image. Daniel and his friends refused to do so. The penalty for such a refusal was death by burning in the furnace. The king gave them a second chance. Daniel replied, "If it be so, our God whom we serve is able to deliver us from the burning fiery furnace, and he will deliver us out of thine hand, O king. But if not, be it known unto thee, O king, that we will not serve thy gods, nor worship the golden image which thou hast set up" (3:17-18).

Once more, later still, a new king, Belshazzar issued a

decree that people might not pray to any god save himself, under penalty of death. Daniel "went into his house; and his windows being open in his chamber toward Jerusalem, he kneeled upon his knees three times a day, and prayed, and gave thanks before his God, as he did aforetime" (6:10). You see, Daniel's habits of body, mind, and spirit stood him in good stead, and saved him when the going was tough. From this character out of the dim past, we can learn.

It is amazing how habits get hold on us. A prisoner who had served his sentence was released, but discovered that he was in bondage to the habits of years spent in a jail cell. When he was set free, he took ten steps outside the cell, turned on his heel automatically, and walked back into it. Ten steps had become for him the limit of life's venture.

Dr. Albert Schweitzer in *On the Edge of the Primeval Forest* tells of some of the strange things about the natives in his section of Africa. At a certain time of year the natives burn off the jungle to clear the ground so they can plant their seeds. Occasionally, unexpected rains make it impossible to burn the growth which must be cleared. When this happens these people simply sit and fold their hands in despair. They could clear the jungle with their hands instead of burning it, but this seems to call for too great an adjustment. Schweitzer says, "They sacrifice their lives rather than exert their bodies." See how habits get hold on us.

Let's take another illustration. One day after closing hours, a woman came into the bank to pay her rent. The only clerk left told her the office was closed, but she insisted on paying anyway. The clerk took the money, and since the vault was already closed, he took it home with him. The next morning, he put on a different suit, and left the money at home. He had to make a false entry in his books to cover it. He told himself that since it was done, he'd wait another day before turning in the money. Finally, he told himself that he was underpaid, and needed the money. The next time the woman came in to pay the rent he took it and kept it, and the next, and the next, until he did it without thinking, that is, until he was caught and charged with embezzlement. The definition of habit is: "A custom or practice, especially an attitude or inclination for some action, acquired by repetition and showing itself in facility or performance or in decreased power of resistance."

When I was a boy, we lived on the farm. A part of our farm lay across some deep woods, and to get to it, we went around a rather long road. Being the lazy sort, I decided one day that it would be easier to go straight through the woods to that section. So I went. There were briars, rocks, bushes, but I pushed them aside and went through. The next time it was easier; the next easier still. When we left that farm, the little path I started had become a road over which the farm trucks could be driven. So a habit begins and continues.

I have never known a man who set out to become a drunkard, only ones who took the first drink, later another, and another, until finally the habit was established. I've never known a man who set out to be a liar. But one falsehood started the habit pattern, and when he told another and another, the pattern became established. I've never known a man to set out to become an adulterer, but one slip of morals, then another, and another, until he had lost his sense of morals. And so it goes. A habit begins with a single decision: the decision to do a thing. The decision settles the matter at hand for the moment. But even more important, that decision makes it likely that you will make the same decision in the future. You do a thing because you want to. Then you do it because you did it before. At the last you do it because you can't help it. By repetition, our attitudes, outlook, and finally our morals are formed.

A four-year-old boy had some trouble with his mother. He

announced that he was leaving home, he just couldn't stand his mother any more. His mother helped him pack and he left. Later a neighbor saw him walking up and down the edge of the street carrying his mother's suitcase and asked, "Where are you going, Jim?" "I'm running away from home," he said. "You won't get very far staying on this side of the street," the neighbor replied. "I know," said Jim, "but I'm not allowed to cross the street."

Habits are subtly formed. Augustine once said: "Because of a forward will, was a lust made; and a lust ever obeyed, became a custom; and a custom, not resisted, brought on a necessity. By which links, as it were, hanging one upon another, for which I have called it a chain, did a very hard bondage me enthrall!" We become what we repeatedly choose. We become a person of integrity or a liar by the decisions we make, and these become habits with us. We become happy persons or somber individuals by choice. Our outlook on life is determined by the choices we make. Success and failure are determined by the habits we choose to form. It all begins with a choice.

As a boy on the farm, one of my favorite little games was to bring in a cucumber in a bottle. The neck would be very small, but the cucumber would fill the bottle. I could almost always fool someone with it. The secret is simple: slip a tiny little cucumber into the bottle soon after the blossom leaves, and let it grow in the bottle. At the last, you can't get the cucumber out. So it is with habits. They grow in us, as a result of a repeated choice.

> Two roads diverged in a yellow wood,
> And sorry I could not travel both
> And be one traveler, long I stood
> And looked down one as far as I could
> To where it bent in the undergrowth;

Then took the other, as just as fair,
And having perhaps the better claim,
Because it was grassy and wanted wear;
Though as for that, the passing there
Had worn them really about the same,

And both that morning equally lay
In leaves no step had trodden black.
Oh, I kept the first for another day!
Yet knowing how way leads on the way,
I doubted if I should ever come back.

I shall be telling this with a sigh
Somewhere ages and ages hence:
Two roads diverged in a wood, and I—
I took the one less traveled by,
And that has made all the difference.
—Robert Frost
"The Road Not Taken"

You become what you repeatedly choose. This applies to bad habits. But by the same token, it applies to good ones, as we shall see. You can be more than you are if you can master the choice of habits. There are several steps which help to destroy a bad habit and create a good one.

(1.) In the first place, decide honestly what your bad habit is. No one ever inherited a bad habit. The evil that besets our lives is acquired evil. The very first step in being rid of such a habit is to face up to it honestly. We have to look carefully at a habit in order to determine the real cause. Here is a man who has become a habitual drinker. It is not something that he wants to do. On close examination, he finds that another problem is at the root of his drinking. He has a problem that makes him want to drink to forget it.

During the last supper Jesus had with his disciples he announced that one of them would betray him. They all began asking, "Is it I?" Judas asked too. He wasn't being a hypocrite. He knew he was the one. But he was talking to himself. "Am I really the kind of person who could do this? Is my character such that I can betray my friend?" He was soul searching. We ought to probe deep into our own lives to discover what makes us form the kind of habits we do. What is my real problem? Drinking, lying, cheating often are but symptoms of a deeper need.

So try honestly to decide what the problem is that causes the habit. Take time to know yourself. Face it.

(2.) The second step is to make up your mind that you want to be rid of the habit, whatever it is. That sounds silly, or easy. But it's not so silly and not so easy either. Some of us get to the point where we like our habits. We are divided in our feelings about this. A part of us will say, "I know this is wrong, and I ought to stop." Another part of us will say, "Yes, but I like it." And such a divided will defeats any possibility of breaking a habit. Make up your mind that you want to stop.

(3.) In the third place, stop. Stop now! Often we know what the habit is, we are convinced that we want to be rid of it, but we keep on putting it off with, "I'll do it soon." But you never do it on that basis. Many a person has told me that about joining the church. "I know I ought to do it. I'm going to do it. But not now."

There is an old story about the devil and his plan to destroy the world. He called in his helpers, and told them his plan. One of them, Anger, said, "Let me go and destroy man. I will set brother against brother. I will get men angry with each other and they will destroy themselves." This did not appeal to the devil. Then Lust spoke. "I will defile men's minds. I will make love disappear and men will be turned into beasts." This was not the answer. Greed said, "I will instill in men's hearts the most destructive force of all. Man's uncontrolled desires will destroy him." Jealousy, Gluttony, Drunkenness, Idleness, Hate all came and presented their plans. But the devil was not satisfied with any one of them. Then came one last helper. He said, "I will go and talk persuasively in terms of all that God wants man to be. I shall tell him how fine his plans are to be honest, clean, brave, pure. I shall encourage him in all the good plans and purposes of life." The devil was aghast at such talk. But his helper hastened on to say, "But I will tell him there is no hurry. Tomorrow will be time enough, and he can do them all then." This helper's name was Procrastination. The devil said, "Go!" And many people, knowing that they ought to decide against a bad habit have said "tomorrow," or "just once more," and found it too late. Stop now!

(4.) But all these are not enough. It is good to know what your habit is, and want to break it, and resolve to stop it now. How many times have you done that only to find that when the opportunity came you did it again? To tell an alcoholic "Use your willpower" is a waste of words if that is all you say. To tell a man who has the habit of hating "Stop hating" is silly if that is all you tell him. We need something that we don't have. We must go one step more. There is a word in the Christian language that has been taken over by industry that we need to recover: conversion. Conversion is the way of release for the person who has a serious habit to break. Conversion provides not only the desired goal in life, but also provides the power for getting there. The secret of breaking a habit is to stop trying to do it ourselves and trust Christ. This is what conversion in the Christian sense means; it means to turn from self-trust to trust in him. Paul said to the Philippian Christians: "I can do all things through Christ which strengtheneth me" (Phil. 4:13). This is the answer. Know what your habit is, want to stop, resolve to stop, surrender your life to Jesus Christ. Often, when this surrender is made, the desire for an old habit disappears immediately and never returns.

Dr. Carl Jung tells of talking with a patient, and advising him to get a Christian faith. The man was cynical and said, "You don't believe that stuff, do you?" Dr. Jung replied, "I am no theologian, but I know one thing—if you get a religious faith you will get well. If you don't, you won't." Here is the vital secret of being rid of any habit that robs us of efficiency, destroys the possibility of happiness, and keeps us from being the people God wants. I can promise that whatever your habit, by a surrender to God, by the process of conversion, by turning your back on wrong actions, wrong attitudes, wrong, choices, and turning to Christ, you can be rid of it.

The beginning of Alcoholics Anonymous is a fascinating story. A man named Bill, a successful stockbroker in New York, became a drunk. He was hopeless in his own eyes and in the eyes of his friends. One morning, he sat in the kitchen drinking, talking with a non-drinking friend. His friend had found help for his drinking problem through faith in God. Bill could not go along with any "God-concept." He rejected that kind of help.

Later that year, he woke up in Towns Hospital, being sobered up. His friend visited him again. Bill was alone later in the day. "I realized that I was powerless, hopeless, that I could not help myself and nobody else could help me. In the midst of this, I remembered this God business. I rose up in bed and said, 'If there be a God, let him show himself now.' All of a sudden, there was a light, a blinding white light that filled the whole room. A tremendous wind seemed to be blowing all around me and right through me. I felt that I stood in the presence of God. I felt an immense joy. And I was sure beyond all doubt that I was free from my obsession with alcohol." Out of this experience Alcoholics Anonymous was born to bless millions of lives.

No one of us is powerful enough to handle our habits alone. I was staying in a lovely home near West Point, Georgia, while guest preacher in West Point First Methodist Church. On the mirror in my bathroom was a sticker with the words, "Let go; let God." I believe that is the answer to handling our habits.

(5.) But we must take another step. After conversion, if we are not to lapse into old patterns again, we must begin to make right choices, and discipline ourselves in good habits. Unless we replace the old ones with new ones the old ones will come trooping back again. Remember Jesus' story of the man whose life was swept free of an unclean spirit? The spirit wandered around, but found no place to rest. He returned to the house from which he came and found it empty. He rounded up other evil spirits, seven more wicked than himself, and they all moved in. ". . . and the last state of that man is worse than the first" (Matt. 12:43-45). We must deliberately employ our energies in the service of the good and right if we are to grow and develop into the kind of character we hope to have.

Old temptations will return. Positive practice in right choices and habits is the answer. One day Christy Mathewson gave a talk on the good life to some young boys. Then he went out on the playground to show them something about baseball. Christy began pitching to the boys. He was a master at curves. No matter where the boy held the glove Christy threw the ball right in it. They asked him the secret of being such a great pitcher. He made a simple statement: "You can do it only when you pitch, and pitch, and pitch, and pitch." A regular, determined practice of good, right choices is the final step in overcoming a bad habit. It is true that God helps those who cannot help themselves. It is also true that he helps those who help themselves.

A little girl said to her mother at bedtime, "Mother, I've had such a happy time today." The mother smiled and said, "Really? What made this day different from yesterday?" The child thought a moment, then said, "Yesterday my thoughts pushed me around and today I pushed my thoughts around." There is a world of wisdom in the child's observation. As long as our habits push us around, we cannot achieve real happiness, or be creative, or be constructive. But when by the grace and strong help of God we get control of our habits, rid ourselves of the bad ones and set in motion new and good ones, then we discover genuine happiness. Happiness is a by-product, a by-product of being right and good and what God wants of us.

10

Born
to Raze Hell

In preparation for this chapter read John 12:27.

I spend a lot of time in my car and find that the radio is a constant companion. (Except that lately I have started listening to cassettes containing sermons, lectures, and special kinds of music!) One morning I turned it on and literally got blasted by someone singing at the top of his voice, "Life is what you do while you are waiting to die!" When that was finished, I changed stations just in time to hear the theme from the Broadway musical, *Man of La Mancha*.

To dream the impossible dream,
   to fight the unbeatable foe,
To bear with unbearable sorrow,
   to run where the brave dare not go.

To right the unrightable wrong,
   to love pure and chaste from afar,

To try when your arms are too weary,
    to reach the unreachable star!

This is my quest, to follow that star,
No matter how hopeless, no matter how far;
To fight for the right without question or pause,
To be willing to march into hell for a heavenly cause!

And I know, if I'll only be true
To this glorious quest, that my heart will
    lie peaceful and calm,
When I'm laid to my rest,
And the world will be better for this;
That one man, scorned and covered with scars,
Still strove with his last ounce of courage,
To reach the unreachable stars.
        —Joe Darion
         "The Impossible Dream (The Quest)"

Contrast two attitudes portrayed by these two songs: "Life is what you do while you are waiting to die!" A man needs "to dream the impossible dream." This musical, *Man of La Mancha*, was not supposed to be very significant. It was another version of the old Don Quixote story. But at the end of the first performance, the audience stood and cheered, and the critics raved and said here was a musical that would last a generation. Why? The words and music tugged at something buried deep in the human heart that most people thought dead: the appeal of a great dream, a tremendous ideal.

We've lost some of this zeal for the ideal. Norman Cousins, editor of *Saturday Review/World,* reported that on one of his visits to Korea, he rode in a jeep with a soldier near the front. When he asked about morale, the soldier replied,

"Well, morale is not just a matter of USO shows and free beer. To have morale you have to be connected up with the folks back home, and connected up with something that really matters. The trouble here is that we aren't connected up."

Every person has two birthdays: the day he is born and the day he discovers why he was born. The second is infinitely more important than the first. The greatest thing that can happen to any one of us is to be touched by some great ideal, some idea that won't let you rest, or some great person who is a challenge, a Saviour who points the way, then leads you into it. Here is why Jesus is so everlastingly important. I may oversimplify this thing of being a Christian, but being one is following Jesus. Someone else has defined being Christian as "accepting Jesus' offer of friendship, then living so as to be worthy of that friendship."

I have learned a lot from the Jesus people, the Jesus freaks, and some of the other very fundamental groups on the college campuses. One Sunday a well-to-do jazz musician went to church, and afterwards met the pastor at the door. "Preacher," he said, "that was a groovy sermon today. You really had me swinging. I almost flipped my lid." "I am most pleased that you liked my sermon," said the dignified minister, "but I would appreciate it if you would not use such low terminology to express your feelings." "Sorry," said the musician, "but I just had to tell you how your message sent me. Why I dug what you said so much that I flipped a C-note in the money pot!" "Cool, man," said the preacher, "cool and crazy!"

The major thing I have learned from these people is to simplify the gospel. Of course, it isn't simple to work out, but in its initial stage in a person's life, the gospel is much simpler than we tend to make it.

Out ahead of him, Jesus could see a cross. He prayed, "Now is my soul troubled. And what shall I say? 'Father, save me from this hour'? No, for this purpose I have come to this hour" (John 12:27, RSV). This lets us see a side of Jesus that is akin to ourselves. We usually see great characters with minds made up, resolute, course set, jaws fixed. Rarely do we see them sweat out uncertainty, or struggle with doubt before seeing the way. This makes Jesus all the more meaningful to us. He said, "Now is my soul troubled." He struggled with the direction his life should take just like you and I do. Then he saw his way clearly, and he said, ". . . for this purpose I have come to this hour. Father, glorify thy name" (John 12:27-28, RSV). He found his purpose for living! And each of us can be more than we are if we find our purpose in life, our reason for being.

We are to be change agents. Kenneth Scott Latourette once said that we don't have one revolution going but five: political, social, economic, educational, religious. How right he was and is. The world around us, and within us, is in a state of change, revolution. Once when we were at a football game at Georgia Tech, during half time a dog got on the field. Time for the game to begin came, and the dog wouldn't come off. From the stands all around came the calls: "Here! Here! Here!" Some of the people calling sounded like they had had experience calling dogs or pigs. But the little dog was confused. He simply stood in the middle of the field and turned around and around. How similar his feelings must have been to ones we so often experience in today's world.

What changes are taking place around us in medicine, transportation, communications, home building, farming, homemaking. There are revolutions everywhere, even in clothing styles. It used to be that a man who hid behind a woman's dress was called a coward. Now he is called a magician. A young man involved in some of the demonstrations in New York recently was asked what he was doing. His reply was that they were destroying the institution. Asked what he would substitute for the institution, he replied, "We haven't decided that yet. We are just destroying what is." Changes everywhere. We must be change agents, too.

We must introduce the spirit of Christ into all the other changes taking place. We must not be for change just for change's sake, but we must be such a change agent that the societies of the world shall become the society of our God. We are to seek by all legitimate means to bring the practices of the world into conformity with truth, the dignity of persons, beauty, hope, and love. We must have and hold tenaciously some convictions about right and wrong, honesty, the worth of people, and seek to bring such changes into human relationships that people will become brothers and sisters, children of one God, and the world a paradise. We are to be change agents.

We are to be establishers of values. A great thing about Jesus was that he knew what mattered and what didn't. He had his values straight. He knew that all value stemmed from God. He knew that character was more important than cash, men than machines, faith than fame, morals than materials. Our values are distorted. We emphasize pleasures, things, success, sex, fame, glamour, ambition. These are all right in their place, but they have become god to a lot of us. Oddly enough, the more securely these values are fixed in our thinking, the more we miss the great meaning of life.

Life is like a shop window. During the night a prankster slipped in and rearranged the price tags on all the merchandise. Cheap things had a high price tag on them; valuable things were priced low. We'd better ask ourselves seriously what matters, on what we have set our hearts. You can be more than you are if you decide what really matters in life. And the world needs the example of some people who know what is valuable.

Winston Churchill told of a sailor who dived into the bay

to save the life of a little boy. Several days afterward, the sailor met the little boy and his mother on the streets of Plymouth. The mother stopped the sailor, and said, "Are you the man who pulled my little boy out of the water?" Expecting some word of gratitude, the sailor said, "Yes, madam." "Then where's his cap?" the mother asked.

What really matters in life? Love matters. Love lasts. It is the eternal value before which all else pales and dies. I don't mean the sloppy sentimental, sex-oriented something we call love. That is not love. It means, "I love me and I want you." Real love implies respect, friendship, brotherhood, a desire for the best for the object of affection, for all people. It is a willingness to get involved in constructive action. It is patient, kind, hopeful. It never fails. On the basis of this kind of love the world moves upward. We must establish love as life's chief value in our own lives, and in the lives of all that we touch. You can be more than you are if you know what matters.

We are to be eradicators of the ugly and establishers of beauty. Abraham Lincoln once said that he'd like to be known as one who plucked a weed and planted a flower wherever he thought a flower would grow. How much ugliness and sordidness there is in the world. Take our highways for example. When you set out to enjoy the mountains and the lakes you can hardly see them for billboards advertising everything from "Jesus Saves" to the nearest honkytonk, from alligators to orange juice, from the next luxury motel to Rock City. A man in Florida saw a sign that said "All the orange juice you can drink for a dime." Realizing that what Anita Bryant says is true (A day without orange juice is like a day without sunshine), he stopped. He paid his dime, drank, and held out the glass for refilling. The man said, "That will be another dime." The fellow angrily pointed to the sign "All the orange juice you can drink for a dime." The owner pointed to the empty glass and said, "That's all you can drink for a dime."

There's ugliness everywhere, in novels, movies, television, advertising. Everywhere the emphasis is on the seamy. I have never understood why realism means the seamy, sordid, unshaven, drunk, the foul-mouthed, the unwashed, the person who runs around with another's wife or husband. Why shouldn't beauty be realism too? Why can't the man who works hard all day, gives good service, comes home to his own wife and children, takes a bath, supports the character-building institutions of the community be called a realist too?

There's beauty in the world. It is a startling thought that however horrible the circumstances, no war, no atrocities, no seaminess, no brutality, no pain can destroy the beauty of a rosy dawn, the glory of a flaming sunset, the song of a mockingbird at three in the morning, the loveliness of a deed of mercy, the look in a mother's face as she bends over a sick child. Viscount Gray heard Campbell McInnes sing some of Handel's music in 1914 when Europe was being torn apart. He wrote: "Europe is in the most terrible trouble it has ever known in civilized times, and no one can say what will be left at the end. But Handel's music will survive." Believe that. Love will survive. Hope will. Truth will. Beauty will. We are to be eradicators of the ugly and establishers of the beautiful.

We are to be seekers after truth. In John Masefield's play, *Good Friday,* an old man is selling Easter lilies. He says:

> Friend, it is over now, the passion, the tears,
> the pains. Only the truth remains.

The discovery of truth is no easy matter. William Lyon Phelps of Yale, a brilliant Christian, wrote in his autobiography: "My religious faith remained in possession of the field only after prolonged civil war with my naturally skeptic mind." The noblest faith has come out of doubt, and progress has come to the world because someone has said, "I doubt that. I can't take any more!"

Many things ought to be doubted. Some current ideas about God ought to be doubted. Some things the church does ought to be doubted. Some pronouncements of the sciences, of education, of the skeptics ought to be doubted. We ought to doubt that war is inevitable, that the white man is better than the black man, that any person is doomed to failure. Truth has come because someone has said, "I doubt that," and has sought truth, even to the sacrifice of life. Just suppose out beyond what you now accept as truth there should be something more. Just suppose. We are to be seekers after truth. And seeking truth, we seek God; finding truth, we find God.

We are to be ones who care. I read "Peanuts" every day and especially on Sundays. In one strip Charlie Brown and Linus watch as their teacher, Miss Othmar, marches in the rain in the teachers' strike. "Poor Miss Othmar," says Linus, "it's raining and she's on strike. I'm bringing her some soup." Miss Othmar falls. Lucy shows up and asks what's going on. Charlie Brown explains that Miss Othmar fell, and that Linus had rushed over to pick up her sign. Lucy shouts, "That blockhead! He's become involved!" Do the needs of the world, the hurts of people cry so loud that it seems as if someone were calling your name? No matter how limited your ability may be, there are ways to get involved. Someone has said that no person is completely worthless: he can at least serve as a bad example. We are to be ones who care.

Some time ago the *New York Times* carried a story about a demonstration among college students in Brazil. It was the kind of demonstration I like. Thousands of them had been out for a month. They had gone into villages and out-of-the-way places in the jungles. They had built more than a thousand houses, and the medical students had treated more than six-hundred-thousand people in various stages of need.

Did you ever see a baby die of starvation? One Saturday afternoon, when I was pastor of an Atlanta church, I was in the office. The telephone rang. It was a request for help for a family that had had no food for days, and since they were newcomers to Atlanta, welfare couldn't help them. I went to a run-down section of the city, within sight of the golden dome of the State Capitol. I parked, and walked half a block. I saw filth, rats running here and there, broken glass, junk. I stepped up on the porch of a house that was ready to fall in. A ragged, unkempt woman answered my knock. She told her story—no work, no food, moving from place to place. The children were hungry, and she was afraid one of them was seriously sick. I went into another room, and on the dirty mattress was a little form, belly distended from hunger, fever high, crying. I went to the nearest telephone and called an ambulance. The baby died on the way to the hospital. We got help for the family. Did you ever see a baby starve to death? Would you care?

There's hurt in the world, hurt that you and I can help. You can be more than you are if you decide to do it!

What am I here to do? Is life what you do while waiting around to die, or is it dreaming the impossible dream? A student told me recently that his goal in life was "to finish college, get a good job, marry a pretty girl, have two fine children, own a nice house in a neighborhood where schools were good, close to the country club so he could play golf and tennis on weekends, have several close friends. . . ." Not a word did he mention about doing anything worthwhile for anyone else. Not a word about caring.

On a hot July night in 1966, Chicago police answered a call to a flophouse. There had been a fight, and one young man was bleeding profusely from a deep cut on his arm. The police gave emergency treatment, then loaded him up, and set out for the county hospital. It was a routine, dirty, nightly job.

The man was taken to the emergency room, and a young resident doctor began to help him. The doctor moistened his finger with saliva and rubbed the patient's left arm. As he rubbed he saw the letter "B" appear. He rubbed some more, wiped the arm clean, and saw the words tattooed on the man's arm, "Born to raise hell!" He called the police, and within minutes this young man was identified as Richard Speck, who three days before had murdered eight nurses in Chicago's worst crime. Richard Speck had faithfully carried out the purpose tattooed on his arm.

"Raise" means to start, create, lift up. A lot of people raise hell all their lives. That seems to be their purpose. We are born to *raze* hell. "Raze" means to destroy, put down, demolish. We are here to raze hell. We are to be servants of God. You can be more than you are!

11

My Name Is Simon . . .

In preparation for my story read Mark 15:15-22.

My name is Simon. I was born in the lovely city of Cyrene
on the southern shores of the Mediterranean. Cyrene is
an old city, built in 630 B.C. It is the capital of Libya, and the
center of a prosperous agricultural area. Our city has been
the center of democracy and culture for nearly four hundred
years. Except for the years away at school, I have spent all
my life in this beautiful city.

My father was Jewish. He fell in love with a beautiful Berber
woman and they were married. There are nearly a million
of us Jews living along the northern coast of Africa. My
father made a fortune in olives and sulphium, and I have
continued to reap the benefits of a good commerce.

The cultural advantages of Cyrene are many. I can read
Greek and Latin as well as my own Hebrew tongue. Here
there is an academy founded in 300 B.C. by Aristippus,
that famed son of Socrates. Greek young people come to us
from over the world to study and this school of philosophy is
a vigorous one. In fact, one of my sons, Alexander, is in school

there now studying the wisdom of Aristippus and Socrates
and his descendants. My other son, Rufus, loves the fields.
He is overseer of the crops and the slaves and the family
fortune. He and Alexander are as different as day and dark.
Alexander is fair of skin like his grandfather and Rufus
is bronzed like his Berber grandmother. Rufus is always
talking about the crops and prices, and is impatient with
Alexander who is deeply interested only in philosophy.

Not long ago I spent some time reading our ancient writings.
I was reading from "The Preacher" (Ecclesiastes). "Then I
commended mirth, because a man hath no better thing
under the sun, than to eat, and to drink, and to be merry: for
that shall abide with him of his labour the days of his life,
which God giveth him under the sun" (Eccles. 8:15). Is that
so? I thought. Is all that one can hope for, to eat and drink
and be merry? I was not happy, though I had great wealth, a
lovely wife, and two fine sons. Somehow I didn't feel as
though I was amounting to anything or doing anything. I
had lost my old fire and joy. I wanted to be more than
I was.

I'd been thinking that I'd like to go up to Jerusalem for
the Passover. I'd been torn between money and the pagan
philosophy my son Alexander was studying, and what I'd
been reading in the ancient law given Moses on Sinai. I
needed something to help me decide what is right and give
me new perspective. I thought, maybe there really is balm
in Gilead. I decided to go to Jerusalem.

My whole family objected. It was twenty-seven days by camel
from Libya to Jerusalem and I wanted to take only one
servant. They protested that it wasn't safe on the desert for
a rich man, what with so many robbers. But I went and I
took only one servant. I joined some others over the caravan
route and we discussed the things we expected to see in the
Holy City. The days were blistering hot, and nights freezing
cold. But suddenly after twenty-seven days we were there!

There was the Mount of Olives. How beautiful the sun was

upon it. And there was the temple—magnificent building!
How light my heart felt though my body was weary. I got
down from my camel and decided to walk with the other
pilgrims the rest of the way to the city. People stared at
me. I was wearing the silk clothes of a wealthy man and they
were in sharp contrast to the dull rags of so many others.
But I didn't care. I pushed along with the singing crowd. It
was like going to a circus. People lined the streets watching
the pilgrims pour in and the pilgrims pushed gaily along,
minds fixed on the joys of the Feast of the Passover.

Suddenly the crowd slowed and the singing stopped. The
people along the road looked grim and restless. Out of
the city gate I saw a squad of Roman soldiers marching
briskly. They came so fast that we barely had time to press
into the crowd along the roadside. Behind them came three
men, each carrying a rough cross hewn out of cedar. They
stumbled and staggered, goaded on by the lashing whips
of their tormentors. They were young men. Two of them
were grizzled of face and hard as nails. They looked like
robbers or revolutionists to me. That third man—the one
with the crown of thorns on his head, blood streaming down
into his eyes—how fair he was. He was no robber. I wondered
what he had done. I looked about. Women gasped in horror at
the brutality of the Roman soldiers. The men standing by
had fierce looks of hate on their faces.

But while I was thinking, the young man with the thorns on
his head came even with me, stumbling and reeling as
though he would fall. A soldier lashed his back open and
blood spurted everywhere. He reeled under the weight
and went down. Then suddenly, I felt heavy hands on me
and two soldiers stood beside me. "Carry that cross!" one
ordered harshly. I didn't move or say a word. What an insult!
Who did they think they were? But there was no time for
philosophical reflection. They threw me under the cross,
and in that moment it happened. My eyes met the eyes of the
young man with the thorns. What eyes! How much love
and pity mingled there. They had a tender look of compassion
and even joy, yet of deep hurt. Something happened within

me and I stood up under the cross and carried it as if it had
been a tent pole. The man staggering from pain at my side
started to speak: "Thank you for bearing . . ." but the
soldier lashed him again and shouted, "Shut up." So we
walked along in silence. But I saw in his eyes a look of
gratitude and love. Suddenly I remembered what Alexander
had said to me in our last conversation before I left home,
"Happiness lies in sharing the joy and pain of another.
Pleasure sometimes consists in self-sacrifice!" But as I thought
we arrived at the ugly place where these three were to be
executed. I still didn't know what they had done. But that
one whose cross I carried—I wondered who he was. Then
in a fleeting moment the words of the Prophet Isaiah raced
through my mind: "The people that walked in darkness
have seen a great light: they that dwell in the land of the
shadow of death, upon them hath the light shined. . . . For
unto us a child is born, unto us a son is given: and the
government shall be upon his shoulder: and his name shall
be called Wonderful, Counsellor, The mighty God, The
everlasting Father, The Prince of Peace. Of the increase of
his government and peace there shall be no end, upon the
throne of David, and upon his kingdom, to order it, and
to establish it with judgment and with justice from
henceforth even for ever. The zeal of the Lord of hosts will
perform this" (9:2, 6-7).

That was it! He was the one for whom we had longed and
looked. Did not Isaiah also say, "Surely he hath borne our
griefs, and carried our sorrows: yet we did esteem him
stricken, smitten of God, and afflicted. But he was wounded
for our transgressions, he was bruised for our iniquities: the
chastisement of our peace was upon him; and with his stripes
we are healed" (53:4-5)? But my reverie was short-lived. The
soldiers, with cursing, pushed me out of the way, and laid
their victim on the cross, and with deft strokes of a maul
they drove nails in his hands, tied his feet to the upright, and
with a shout lifted the cross, and with a sickening thud
thrust it into its place in the ground. Finished with their
gruesome task, they broke the legs and arms of the other two

victims to hasten death, but this man, they opened his side with a spear.

In a daze I wandered around and found several people standing talking and watching. I remember hearing someone call one of them Mary Magdalene. I asked her who he was. She thanked me for carrying his cross and then said softly, "He is Jesus, the Son of God, and our Master!" "Our Master!" Then I saw him move his head and I knew he was about to speak. I rushed to hear and fell back amazed for he said, "Father, forgive them for they know not what they do." He said more, but I didn't hear it. I realized he must be God's Son, the Messiah, the one for whom we had waited and longed these centuries. And even as I said it, I felt a strange sensation in my soul and I loved him. I knew I had found the answer to my questing, and I cried out, "My Lord and my God." And then he was dead. I stayed and watched them bury him, and then wandered around the city listening to the talk about what had happened.

Came Sunday and the news spread like wildfire that he was alive. I joined some of his disciples and they welcomed me for what I had done. And joy of joys, he came to us in a closed room. I saw the nail prints and the riven side. I heard him speak. I saw him often in the days that followed. I was there on that memorable day when in Galilee he said to us, "Go ye therefore, and teach all nations, baptizing them in the name of the Father, and of the Son, and of the Holy Ghost: Teaching them to observe all things whatsoever I have commanded you: and, lo, I am with you alway, *even* unto the end of the world" (Matt. 28:19-20). And I was there when he said to Peter, "Feed my sheep" (John 21:17). And I was there that day when he went away from us to heaven. I remember his words, "But tarry ye in the city of Jerusalem, until ye be endued with power from on high" (Luke 24:49*b*). And he was gone. And yet I didn't feel that he was gone at all, so real was his presence in my soul. He was right with me!

I stayed with the disciples during that long forty-day period as we prepared for the thing Jesus had told us to do. Then it happened. We were in an upstairs room, praying, wanting more than life itself to have Jesus with us. Suddenly there was a sound like the wind howling over the desert, and my brain felt like it was on fire, and I wanted to speak. We all started speaking, each of us in his own native dialect. There I heard Peter preaching to them and saying, "God hath made that same Jesus, whom ye have crucified, both Lord and Christ" (Acts 2:36b).

A month later I was back home in Cyrene. I found my family worried about my safety and they expected tales of danger and hazard on the desert. Rufus babbled about the price of olives and sulphium. Alexander talked of a new teacher at the academy. I could hardly wait until supper was over. Then as the moon rose full over the city, I told them what had happened. When I finished I said, "My loves, I have found that for which I have sought these many years. My heart is at peace. I have found the Messiah. I have joined the movement."

Then I turned to Alexander and said: "Son, do you remember our discussion before I left in which you quoted an ancient philosophy that 'Pleasure consists sometimes in self-sacrifice and that to share the joy or pain of another is the real source of happiness'?" Alexander said softly, "Yes, Father, I remember." "Well, my son, I have found that true. Cross-bearing is life's highest joy. Never have I known quite the happiness I found in sacrificing my position and wealth and humbling myself to take on my shoulders the cross of this man. He was suffering, dying; he needed me. I gave myself to him and in that moment, the look of gratitude in his face repaid me for all I had ever done. There is no joy or peace apart from sacrificial love and self-giving for the hurts and pains of others.

"And while I was in Jerusalem I saw the slums, the slaves, the lost and lonely people, the sick by the Pool of Bethsaida. I saw little children deserted. I saw hunger—gaunt women hugging starving babies against flat breasts. I saw all the

horrors of war, men mangled and maimed, and families left
fatherless. I saw drunk men. I met a prodigal who had
run away from home. He was destitute and was eating out of
garbage cans. I saw women violated and treated like animals
right in the street. There were robbers in the desert. I saw
gambling at the foot of the cross. I talked with young men
studying at the university who are dabbling with pagan
philosophy and I saw the hunger and emptiness in their eyes.

"I have become a follower of Jesus; my family and I have
discovered that cross-bearing, self-sacrifice, to share the
joy and pain of another, is life's highest joy. I heard Jesus say
one day, 'For whosoever will save his life shall lose it; but
whosoever shall lose his life for my sake and the gospel's,
the same shall save it' (Mark 8:35). I cannot just sit and enjoy
my wealth, and spend my time dozing and reading when all
the world is dying. And so I am going to sell my estates,
give to each of you your rightful share and use my money
and my days in the service of my king. I am going to give my
energy and time to relieve suffering and to tell the story
of what Jesus has done for me! I wish you would join me in
this the highest endeavor in life, for there is a place for us
all. Nothing I have ever found has brought the satisfaction
that carrying a man's cross brought me. So I shall spend my
days in cross-bearing.

"One thing more—Jesus belongs to all people and he can
satisfy the deepest longings of every person. You know I am a
half-breed—half Jew, half Berber. But he loves me and
fulfills my needs. He makes me more than I ever dreamed I
could be. He cleansed and healed two people caught up
in the throes of sexual promiscuity. He saved a Samaritan
woman by the well. He is for all races and all creeds and all
philosophies. He brings unity between diverse men. At
Pentecost, I saw people from nearly every country changed
and empowered by his spirit. I believe he is the answer to
human emptiness and lostness, to the things that divide
people and make them enemies, to youth's quest for deepest
truth and highest good, to woman's search for selfhood. I
believe him to be the answer to war and drink and wrong

uses of sex. Son, I believe he is the answer for all people and for all that people are seeking. I believe he can make every person more than he is! And so I have given my life to him, to go on bearing his cross until I shall lie with my fathers in sleep. For I know now that real pleasure consists in self-sacrifice and that to bear the joy and sorrow of another is the real source of happiness!"

My name is Simon!

If I'm So Free, How Come I Feel Boxed In? by Dennis Guernsey (#0066–2). Dennis Guernsey offers a horizon-expanding look at the real possibilities of understanding and accepting the freedom available to all in Christ.

Learn to Live with Style by Eileen Guder (QP #2823–0). Insights and guidelines for living the Christian lifestyle—a lifestyle which is easily identifiable, uniquely rewarding, and ultimately fulfilling. A thorough sketch of the facets of the Christian "style"—Love, Joy, Gentleness, and many others.

Stages by John R. Claypool (#0034–4). Here is a well-drawn roadmap for the journey upon which all humans find themselves—the journey of life. Using the tempestuous life of the Bible's David, John Claypool shows scripturally and reasonably the true art of "living the expected."

Living, Loving and Letting Go by John C. Cooper (#0014–X). Here is a sensitive manual for parents which follows many of their children's problems and questions from the childhood years to the day when the parents realize that their children are young adults. An excellent foundation book for parents of all ages.